The Love Contract

*Give crowns and pounds and guineas
But not your heart away.*

—A. E. Housman

The Love Contract

HANDBOOK FOR A LIBERATED MARRIAGE

Robert E. Burger

 VAN NOSTRAND REINHOLD COMPANY
New York Cincinnati Toronto London Melbourne

Van Nostrand Reinhold Company Regional Offices:
New York Cincinnati Chicago Millbrae Dallas

Van Nostrand Reinhold Company International Offices:
London Toronto Melbourne

Copyright ©1973 by Litton Education Publishing, Inc.

Library of Congress Catalog Card Number: 72-14035
ISBN: 0-442-21470-7

All rights reserved. No part of this work covered by the
copyright hereon may be reproduced or used in any form or by any
means—graphic, electronic, or mechanical, including photocopying,
recording, taping, or information storage and retrieval systems—
without permission of the publisher.

Manufactured in the United States of America

Published by Van Nostrand Reinhold Company
450 West 33rd Street, New York, N.Y. 10001

Published simultaneously in Canada by Van Nostrand Reinhold Ltd.

15 14 13 12 11 10 9 8 7 6 5 4 3 2 1

Library of Congress Cataloging in Publication Data

Burger, Robert E
  The love contract.

  1. Marriage—United States. I. Title.
HQ536.B86   301.42'0973   72-14035
ISBN 0-442-21470-7

For T., with love.

ACKNOWLEDGMENT

The author wishes to thank several friends for their valuable assistance: Mike Hamilton and Paul Allman editorially and Wee Russell for manuscript preparation.

Introduction – the Liberated Marriage

"Liberation" has become a fighting word in our society. The more general concept of freedom is likewise no longer the lofty, abstract ideal of Fourth of July oratory. We publicly demand the release of political activists from the clutches of the courts; we boycott stores and corporations to gain more "liberal" labor contracts. If the women's lib movement had a slogan, it might be "Free the American Hundred Million."

This sort of liberation assumes an obvious oppressor—whether capitalism or male chauvinism or religious taboos. Yet there is no oppressor quite as brutal as that unseen villain, ignorance, in its many guises: self-doubt, pride, misunderstanding, deceit, mistrust, fear. And the conqueror of ignorance is *communication*.

We have all heard this recipe before. "Communicate and all will be well." It is the message of a dozen current "marriage books." Why another one? Why another analysis of what goes wrong in marriage and how matters can be remedied?

Why? Because this book is not an analysis—it is a plan of action. It is an exhortation to do something. It is based on the simple psychological fact of behavior that *the fastest way to make a mental change is to make a physical change.* In the case of marriage, the fastest way to make the nuptial contract work is to *write* a contract.

As we will see in the course of this book, "writing" a contract takes many forms—from love letters to legal documents. But the theme behind each form of agreement is the idea that *self-knowledge* is the basic freedom man possesses. This is what liberates an individual; it is what liberates a marriage. All of the forms of communication we know—some of them apparently odious, such as required instruction in the religion of a marriage partner—contribute to the liberation of the human psyche.

It would not be worth repeating this message here again, except for the fact that all of our present advice and our past tradition has led us to believe that love and love alone is the answer. Freely given, no conditions asked, love conquers all. Indeed, the ultimate expression of the Christian ethic is blind love. As all rules and prescriptions are reducible to the Golden Rule, what else is needed?

So it might seem that this book is an argument against romantic love, in favor of a calculating affection. Not true. Just as knowledge tends to liberate rather than confine, love flowers in honesty. This book is an argument for good fertilizer.

Some contracts assure *performance,* as in an agreement to build a house in a given time for a given amount. Other contracts provide for the distribution of money, or the separation of duties, such as in a partnership. The marriage contract is a mixture of both as it now stands in our legal tradition and current legislation. We can improve on that contract in two ways. First, we can recognize all the psychological and emotional agreements that two lovers (and ostensibly two marriage partners) already are making with each other; from these more consciously formulated agreements can evolve. Second, we can draw up formal contracts which, though limited severely by current interpretations of the marriage contract in state law, can at least focus the attention of the prospective bride and groom on what they are really getting into.

But above all this, the concept of a contract has a certain liberating power in itself. It gives us a new way of looking at a very tired and over-talked subject. It allows us to approach an emotional involvement without feeling forced to approach it in an *emotional* way. In this very basic sense, the idea of a contract starts us off on the right foot.

Why should a marriage be liberated? This is another, prior question that deserves an answer. It is all to easy to say simply that we have to accept rules in life, that we must limit our freedom to allow for the freedom of others, and that it is just the human condition to have to struggle under oppressive institutions. My answer to this parade of half-truths is that the finest thing in life is love, and love must be allowed to grow in marriage if it can anywhere. The cynics have already assumed that marriage stifles love, is the death of love. This book argues that the marriage contract is the cradle of love. Because it is love that all the compacts and agreements in this book are designed to protect, I call the totality of these "the love contract."

The enemy of love is not hate, but indifference. Perhaps this little exhortation against indifference can open a few eyes and a few hearts to the love that sets us free.

R. E. Burger

Contents

	Introduction	vii
1	SIGN UP FOR FREEDOM	1
2	WHEREAS, I LOVE YOU	9
3	LOVE LETTERS	15
4	DIALOGUE: THE SPOKEN CONTRACT	21
5	THE SECRET CONTRACT	26
6	THE RITES OF LOVE	38
7	VALUE ADDED BY LOVE	51
8	FREEDOM FROM MONEY	60
9	WRITE YOUR OWN TICKET	72
10	IS MONOGAMY OBSOLETE?	78

1 Sign Up For Freedom

Why would anyone want to sign a contract for the most personal and freely accepted agreement in life: the union of two people in marriage?

This book is an extended answer to this question. A convincing answer to "Why a contract?" is not simply that it is useful, or instructive, or liberating, but how it can be all of these things and to what extent. At the end I will come to the conclusion, and I hope the reader will also, that a contract is a surprisingly effective catalyst for love—in every sense of the word. It is emotionally and psychologically freeing, it is far more instructive than anything else one might do to prepare for marriage, and for these two reasons alone it is highly useful.

We begin with a paradox: can love and legalisms mix? Ever since the age of chivalry, the ideal of romantic love as the basis for marriage has been a consistent theme of Western civilization. It is only because this theme is now so deeply rooted that we can laugh at our own deviations from it, such as marriages arranged by parents or by social registers. We know our values well enough that we spontaneously cheer the triumph of romantic love over the plotting of matchmakers, and we think it is the greatest of good fortune when the protagonists of a play or film, thrown together by blind fate or by scheming relatives, fall madly in love.

We know that marriage and its obligations are very much written into the law. But we instinctively resist the intrusion of "legalities" into the agreement; we are annoyed even by the necessity for blood tests and waiting periods. It has become almost commonplace to devise one's own ceremony, to free it from the rigidity and the "old-fashioned" values of traditional forms. And we associate the uses of the law and of the courts not with marriage but with its dissolution.

Few married couples are aware of the implications of the contract they sign, in effect, when they say "I do." It is as if they don't want to be aware of lawyers and statutes and courts at a time as personal and precious as this. When a woman agrees to "love, honor, and obey," she (rightly) considers the words more symbolic than legally binding. We all assume we know what marriage entails, almost by instinct.

And when we turn to the types of contracts that are specifically drawn up by married couples to augment the requirements of the state, it would seem that they tend to poison the very relationships that they are designed to protect. Consider three basic examples: the financial arrangement, the religious agreement, and the "women's lib" contract, for want of a better name.

The type of marriage contract which has the longest history and the most widespread use is a contract for the division of funds and the disposition of property. Technically known as an "antenuptial agreement" or a "marriage settlement," such a contract is really not *about* marriage at all. As the prefix "ante" suggests, it is an agreement made in *advance* of the customary marriage contract made at the altar or before a justice of the peace—the "I do." It is not prior in time alone; it is on a separate logical level. It is an agreement to make an agreement. In a typical marriage settlement, a man agrees to confer a certain amount of his property on a woman, in return for which she agrees to marry him (and of course to abide by all the terms of the marriage contract established in common law and by statute). Let's consider first why this apparent "purchase" of wife has always had firm legal approbation.

In the field of contracts, the law allows the greatest freedom to make concessions to another party on matters where there is a wide range of personal discretion. In Roman law and later in the common law of England, the greatest latitude is accorded to individuals in how they dispose of their property and how they choose a marriage partner. It is precisely because a person has the widest range of choices in both cases that he can legally "bargain" one for the other. In a contract, one agrees to perform some act or turn over some property *in consideration for* something else of value. The "consideration" in the case of a marriage settlement is, of course, marriage. This consideration is legally so strong that in recent times even parents could effectively offer it on behalf of their children and make it stand up in court. Times are changing.

About the only restrictions on a marriage settlement are (1) that it be in writing, and (2) that it not violate existing provisions in the law for wills, trusts, and the management of funds—which vary from state to state, as we shall see. The financial agreement need not be a fifty-fifty split; typically, it is just the opposite (and this is the reason for the agreement). A wealthy widow may specify that her husband-to-be shall receive only a monthly stipend, or that certain inherited real estate shall be in her name only, and so forth. A sensational rumor spread by an alleged ex-steward of Aristotle Onassis' yacht had it that Jacqueline Kennedy was "limited" to $600,000 a year for maintenance and $100,000,000 as an inheritance, among other rather fanciful provisions. In publishing terms of this dubious contract in Ms. magazine, Susan Edmiston called attention to the stipulation of "separate bedrooms" as something to "spur our imaginations to greater possibilities of contract making."

The fact that antenuptial agreements must be in writing and recorded in the county courthouse, along with such things as papers of incorporation, leads to the interesting voyeuristic possibility of looking up the documents for one's amusement. Don't bother: you will have to search a long time before you come upon anyone you know, and you can find better gossip in the daily newspaper. Certainly you are not likely to come across stipulations about separate bedrooms.

Lawyers tend to be cynical about marriage settlements. Typically, they say, it's the case of a senile gentlemen and a devoted nurse. When a man's relatives (and potential heirs) learn of an impending marriage between the two, they convice him of the wisdom of drawing up an agreement to protect his assets from misuse. A short time after the marriage, the wife files for divorce on the grounds of cruelty. As evidence of cruelty, she cites the fact that she was beguiled into signing a financially onerous contract, whose terms were a constant reminder of her status.

Many marriage settlements, on the other hand, are quite innocent and even reassuring. When an excessive amount of money is in the family or person of one of the parties, it is not only the relatives who may be worried. Both bride and groom will be under a psychological handicap. The misunderstandings which such an inequity between the parties can produce are the tools-in-trade of playwrights. The man who finds "a million-dollar baby in a five and ten cent store" is more likely to win the honest affections of said baby if he can disguise his own financial position. And if he lets it slip that he has an estate on Long Island, and his beloved turns away in anticipation that *he* knows that *she* knows, what can be done, except to call in a Jewish mother? It would be an anticlimax to solve everything with a contract, but I suggest that in real life it has considerable advantages.

First off, more and more financial agreements as time goes on will not have the implication that they are designed to protect either party's *finances*. They protect only their *attitudes* towards finances. To paraphrase Hemingway's old retort to the statement, "The rich are not like you and me," I would say, "No, they're afraid of money." Inherited money, espeically, is often feared for the supposed responsibility it brings. To touch the principal is to erode a sacred trust. On a lesser scale, the value of personal possessions, heirlooms, real estate with sentimental value, and so forth can have equally strong psychological pressure on the one who holds them. Antenuptial agreements about any such property in which one party has a special interest would help to eliminate misunderstandings—not only about the motivation for one's marriage, but more importantly in all future discussions about the property.

In the latter part of this book I suggest that financial aggreements have perhaps the greatest potential for rescuing the institution of marriage. The reasons for this conclusion are simple: (1) money is the major stumbling block in maintaining the stability of marriages (I leave it to the Epilogue to consider whether stability is desirable or even possible in modern society); (2) the precedents for financial contracts are well established in the law, so that their further extension is not any impractical dream; and (3) financial agreements *need not* become bogged down in the general controversy over women's rights, since both the law and public opinion—which is to say the same thing—are less hampered in this area than in any other aspect of "women's lib."

Although superficially discouraging from their past history, financial agreements have every chance of becoming a liberating feature of the normal marriage contract.

The second example of how contracts have extended the usual marriage agreement is in the field of religion. It used to be quite common for a non-Catholic to have to agree, before marrying a Catholic, that he or she would raise any offspring "in the Church." A prescribed course of study for the non-Catholic was also required. Many Catholic jurisdictions insist upon premarital discussions for both parties, even if both are Catholic—"Cana Conferences"—before permission to marry in the Church will be granted. It might be argued that such requirements do not restrict the parties to a marriage, because a civil ceremony is always open for them. But the practical effect of a prohibition by Church authorities on a sincere believer is tantamount to a denial of other options.

It is my experience that religious prescriptions illustrate a major advantage of a contract, but little else: people tend to take more seriously what they are "required" to do—whether they ever intend to do it or not at the time, or whether or not it is legally binding.

The ineffectuality of religious contracts, in other than psychological terms, is underscored by the fact that they can seldom be enforced. A man who refuses to raise children in the religion he has promised can thumb his nose at his "agreement," because a marriage cannot be invalidated over this point except in the rarest of circumstances. In the Catholic Church, one would have to prove that the husband never intended to agree to these terms, in short, that his agreement was fraudulent.

Cana Conferences, for this reason, are a more constructive and honest effort at stabilizing marriages. As we shall see, actual, effective marriage contracts can grow out of such "conferences."

A third type of marriage contract, one that has a shorter history than either the marriage settlement or stipulations about religion, is what might be called the "women's lib" agreement. The underlying assumption of such a contract is that our marriage laws are male-oriented (to put it mildly), that they promote "the notion of wife as dependent and inferior," and that no woman in her right mind would agree to marriage as it now stands on the books if she took the trouble to "read the fine print."

Such is the opinion of Susan Edmiston, writing in the first issue of Ms. magazine. Even allowing for the particular point of view that one might expect in these circumstances, there is no denying that her intentions are quite serious. She recounts the sporadic attempts at writing personal marriage contracts from the time of Mary Wollstonecraft, "that first feminist of us all," whose *A Vindication of the Rights of Women* was published in 1792, down to the Uniform Marriage and Divorce Act, which is currently grinding its long, slow turn through state legislatures. Perhaps the high-water mark in serious challenges to the inequities of marriage laws was reached with the publication of Lucy Stone and Henry Blackwell's contract in 1855. The essence of their agreement was that marriage is a partnership of equals, a commonplace sentiment today. The Lucy Stone League is a fitting way of memorializing her efforts a century and a quarter later.

Some discrimination should be made, however, between those who oppose the anti-feminist aspects of the marriage vows and those who just don't like the institution itself. Edmiston quotes with apparent approval marriage contracts designed, among other things, to establish separate residences for the spouses (Wollstonecraft-Godwin, Sanger-Slee).

What is most interesting about such agreements is that they never seem to have been challenged, even though they are in obvious violation of "public policy." The reason they aren't challenged is that, despite much hand-wringing over the state's role in the marriage laws, public officials simply do not go out looking for trouble in this highly personal field. What does it mean to say that such a contract "wouldn't stand up in court"? A contract is put to the test only when one party wishes to break it, or brings suit because the other party is not fulfilling his or her part of the bargain. Let us suppose that Mr. Slee decided he did not wish to maintain a separate residence, but wished to cohabitate with Margaret Sanger. Would Mrs. Sanger (she retained her first husband's name) try to enforce her contract with Slee, or would not the whole agreement go by the boards with a simple divorce?

A contract which can be dissolved at will, without loss on either side, is weak indeed. This final example brings us to the crux of the variety of proposals for marriage contracts: if there is an insufficient "consideration" that either party brings to the agreement, there really isn't much of a contract.

In modern times, when "irreconcilable differences" are grounds for divorce in more and more states, in varying degrees, the ultimate consideration of the marriage contract is swept aside. That consideration, of course, is "to have and to hold, from this day forward, in sickness and in health, for richer or for poorer," etc. To put the matter another way, marriage is becoming less and less a contract in the traditional meaning of the word.

The traditional, legal analysis of the marriage contract is that the married couple owe each other emotional and physical support, including appropriate financial support, nursing care, companionship, sexual gratification, and "probably" progeny. Supposedly, these terms are unchangeable. One cannot bargain with them as in the case of a financial agreement. One cannot agree to remain celibate, for whatever reason, and married. In line with other contracts, however, it is conceivable that the couple could *extend* the terms of the contract, rather than limit it. For example, the couple could sign an agreement to have sexual intercourse on a regular schedule, or to spend more time together. It is significant that they could agree, in the opinion of many lawyers, to share their financial burdens equally. At one stroke, such a simple agreement would put to rest the fears of feminist groups that the law perpetuates a master-slave economic relationship. The economy, but not the law.

So we see that the first feeble attempts at marriage contracts are neither very effective nor very desirable. The marriage settlement is really not about marriage at all—marriage is just one of the considerations in an otherwise business "deal." The religious contract is purely psychological in an inhibiting way rather than a liberating sense—but it does suggest new ways of breaking down old taboos. And the "women's lib" contract is little more than a publicity release, signed by the espoused, to broadcast their feelings.

Having said all this, I contend that the idea of a contract can be the salvation of the institution of marriage (desirable or not). And that the physical process of signing is as important to a marriage contract as it is to a treaty. The ritual of agreements may indeed be all that is left of the marriage contract—but it could be enough.

The potential of an individual is less than half the potential of two individuals working together. This is the meaning of freedom, to be able to work to one's potential. In the following I want to develop this connection—between signing up and becoming free, between "giving in" and growing, between "legalisms" and love.

2 Whereas, I Love You

The dessert dishes are being taken away, coffee is served, and eight middle-aged men and women, paired with one another as it so happens, have reached that earthen bottom of the evening's conversation which only a combination of broken down reserve and alcoholic exhaustion can produce. "If a man or a woman of forth-five can make a better deal," says one, "why *shouldn't* I?"

"Your Freudian slip is showing, dear. Now why don't you add the usual bit about the children being old enough so they won't be hurt?"

A third, peace-making type interrupts, "Nonsense! You're both taking the easy way out. And that's what's wrong with all this talk about easy divorce and trial marriages and alternative marriages. Three people. Ye Gods! Marrying the faithful nurse! Douglas making a fool of himself with a woman a third his age!"

"You forgot to mention Ford and Rockefeller, dear."

"I say it's no solution. If marriages aren't working out, improve them, don't encourage every yokel to break them up."

And so on into the night. When is an institution worth preserving at heavy cost, and when is it time to change the institution?

What can we do to make marriage a better contract, or can we replace it with new contracts?

The current tendency in society at large, with growing support from the theorists, is to change the institution. Whether this shift is a cultural phenomenon of our age, just a temporary see-saw from the norm of monogamy, is a question the Epilogue considers. For now let's consider how we might preserve the institution of marriage, or, better, preserve *love* in marriage—at the "heavy cost" of rewriting the marriage contract. The Equal Rights Amendment to the Constitution, which is slowly gathering the necessary votes state by state for ratification, will not appreciably alter personal relationships that never come to a court of law—as they do in divorce or inheritance cases.

Much of the *talk* about marriage contracts, to use the dinner table parlance of our friends, is just "the easy way out."

"Why should marriage be any different from any other contract," is the way the question is usually put. In asking this precise question, Kristin Booth Glen of the New York University Law School means to put marriage contracts as enforced by the states to the test of Article I, Section 10 of the Constitution, which prohibits states from impairing the obligations of contracts.

Marriage *is* different from most other contracts, however, in that it involves *public policy* on a pervasive scale. The success or failure of millions of individual marriages is important to the structure of society, even to the survival of the nation. This fact is underlined by the way in which economic changes from one generation to the next have forced changes in the marriage contract. In the nineteenth century, public policy in this country favored a high birth rate. Thus an agreement not to have children would not have been enforceable, and probably would have invalidated a marriage. Today, such an agreement might well stand up. We have not quite reached the full swing of the pendulum, in our quest for zero population growth, whereby an agreement in the other direction—to have ten children, for example—would likewise nullify a marriage. The point is this, however: the marriage contract cannot be dismissed as a simple agreement between two parties.

Without undue romanticism it might also be argued that marriage is different from other contracts in that it is the antithesis of *quid pro quo*. The heart of a contract is something given for something received. Yet "Love bears with all things, believes all things, hopes all things, endures all things." Love is not given in exchange for protection, or security, or position—it is given only in exchange for love. The question which has yet to be answered satisfactorily is whether the obvious inequities in the marriage contract as presently written into the law are actually used by men as a class against women as a class. Are women giving more than they are receiving? Are men using the law to enhance their supposed financial superiority? Since it is our common experience that forces *outside* of marriage are the major pressures dictating the roles of men and women as "providers" and "housewives," do men consider this to be part of the "bargain" they freely choose in marriage? And providers are not necessarily controllers, as we well know. Regardless of what the law says, in the daily management of household funds the more worldly-wise tends to take the lead, no matter who brings home the bacon. Is *this* ever part of the bargain?

So before we rush to the easy assumption that (1) marriage is a poorly written contract as it now exists; (2) whole classes of people are being abused by the contract provisions; therefore, (3) if we rewrite the contract we will save whole classes of people from abuse; before we glibly acknowledge this, let us consider how things actually *are*.

I take as an unabashed premise the idea that love is such a strong motivating force that under quite normal circumstances no stipulation, no promise of earthly reward or punishment, is its equal. This is not something I want to believe. I think it's the way things are. Whatever tradition we admire—and tradition is not a fantasy but the residual idealism of us all—whether it be St. John or Sir Thomas Moore or Galileo or Dr. Tom Dooley, respectively in love with a leader or with duty or with the truth or with humanity—the strongest motivating factor seems to be the commitment of love of one sort or another. We find the same blind fascination (or whatever paraphrase there is for "love") in the mother who scrubbed floors to buy her son's freedom ("Call Northside 777"), in a sister who wrote a letter to a daily newspaper on learning of the death of her brother in Vietnam, taking the pains to describe him as a rubber-limbed boy perpetually contorted in mid-air off a diving board, or in less exaggerated contrast in our parents and in ourselves. We may dismiss it as emotion, as "true believing," but we know that the central force is something that "bears with all things, believes all things, hopes all things, endures all things"—some of the time.

The callousness of some of the current attempts at marriage contracts seems to be due to an unwillingness to try to find a place for love in the bargain. A well-publicized contract, the "Shulman Marriage Agreement," Copyright 1970, 1971, by Alix Shulman, is honest to the point of being embarrassing. For example, "... calling doctors, checking symptoms; getting prescriptions filled; remembering to give medicine; taking days off to stay home with sick child, providing special activities. This must be worked out equally, since wife now seems to do it all. In any case, wife must be compensated." Even sadder is this contract provision, the reductio ad absurdum of the search for equality: "Husband is free all Saturday, wife is free all Sunday."

We need constant reminders that the freedom from obligations is quite a different thing from the freedom to be one's self. A liberated marriage does not result from a minute division of duties, in order that you "know where you stand;" a liberated marriage comes from not even having to consider, and hence be bogged down in, minutiae. When the central motivating force of a marriage (love!) is given full rein, agreements follow without being spoken, or, we should say, husband and wife become a living agreement. The ticking off of what each person is *allowed* to do is a sign that the marriage is regarded as a restricting and not a liberating institution.

It is the "minor premise" mentioned above that I claim is open to question: whole classes of people are being abused by the contract provisions of our marriage laws. I think the evidence all around us is that the marriage contract as presently written is hardly the villain, the reason why women seem to be getting the short end of the stick. The whole framework of modern society since the Industrial Revolution has dictated the roles of men and women; nothing in the marriage vows has been responsible. So to change the marriage agreement will not begin to reverse centuries of economic direction. Even worse, by giving the illusion of change without budging the underlying forces, a facile division-of-household-duties contract may only serve as the rug under which the same old problems are swept.

The inequities imposed on women by our traditional interpretation of marriage are tersely summarized by Susan Edmiston: "The bargain in today's unwritten marriage contract is that the husband gets the right to the wife's services in return for supporting her." In developing how this "bargain" works to the financial disadvantage of women, however, Edmiston fails to pinpoint actual grievances. "Economic dependency," she argues, "breeds other kinds of dependency. The woman who has no established right in the family income fares better or worse depending on how well she pleases the head of the household."

In terms of death rates, control of wealth, divorce settlements, and use of time, however, it is usually agreed that wives are hardly inconvenienced by the conventional pattern of marriage. Accordingly, the psychological "dependency" might well be just the reverse of what Edmiston claims. This whole line of argument, based on economic values and the subservience of both parties to financial accomplishment as a measure of worth, only suggests that we should revise our *value* system rather than the marriage contract. When Norman Mailer observes that his work is worth more than housework, he is probably right—in the same sense that life is greater than what sustains it.

There is no common ground of comparison. We can only compare the *levels* on which housework and "real work" rest, by some subjective standard of our own which is always open to change. To most people, a book is worth more than a well-scrubbed floor. To a given person, the well-scrubbed floor could be beyond value. But in general, books are worth more than floors—to most of us.

The fact that financial success is highly prized by both men and women, in and out of marriage, rightly or wrongly, should neither embarrass men nor work to the disadvantage of women. Values are the responsibilities of those who make them—and they are made by people. For all their uses, contracts will not change human nature.

The ultimate example of a relative value is love. What a "consideration" it is in a contract that one person professes his love for another! How can the beloved offer anything commensurate with this term? I think the beauty of the traditional marriage ceremony is a reflection of the attempt to describe, almost in poetic terms, an equivalent for love. The finality, the grandiloquence, the gross exaggeration of the marriage ritual are perhaps best understood as poetry, not as legality. Which is to say, in a paradoxical sense, it is all the more binding.

A value system that is a hand-me-down of archaic theories survives today in the "common-law" property laws of eight states. The states are easier to remember geographically than historically: Washington, Idaho, Nevada, California, Arizona, New Mexico, Texas, Louisiana. In these states, as we shall see, there are certain advantages to be gained from knowing the tax and inheritance laws. The only point I wish to make here is that even though there are substantial differences between these eight states and the other forty-two on matters of money, there are no discernible differences in how marriage has survived as an institution in one group of states as opposed to the others. In the marriage contract, love is the first "whereas," and ultimately, I will argue, the only "whereas" that matters.

3 Love Letters

It is no longer fasionable for lovers, least of all, married couples, to carry on extensive correspondence with each other. Largely because of the telephone, we no longer write; because of television, we no longer read. Ball point pens make the little writing we do psychologically unrewarding; paperbacks make the little reading we do seem cheap and transitory. In our modern illiteracy, however, the deprivation most keenly felt is our inability to express ourselves on a personal level: in short, our inability to write letters.

Brutus Hamilton, track and field coach for many years at the University of California, startled reporters at the 1956 Olympics by revealing a voluminous exchange of letters with his wife back in Berkeley. Here indeed was an old fashioned gentleman. When his correspondence was later published in book form, astonishment must have turned to envy; for here was communication between a man and a woman that a novelist could not hope to duplicate.

Correspondence between authors and editors, between politicians and statesmen, between artists and their lovers have always been a staple of the publishing business. Perhaps not the most finished, but the most revealing writing is in this genre, for the simple reason that good writing results from talking as if to a single person.

Nothing is quite as personal as a love letter and, whether it is written by a philosophy professor or a truck driver, the search for that elusive expression of love totally exposes the writer, as it does the poet. Angela Davis did not write to George Jackson with one eye on a published contract. When her love letters were partially revealed in court, they demonstrated less about "motivation" for a crime than they did about her basic human qualities. It is because love letters are so deeply revealing of one's innermost self that they can be considered the ideal form of a contract, where love is part of the bargain.

Love letters can be used in legal proceedings and have been. I would like to propose going one step further: try writing love letters, not so much for their own sake, but as a way of writing a contract.

A poem is a succinct love letter. I would encourage love poems, too, but for the low repute in which the "modern, scientific mind" holds this form of communication. I offer this test for those who are not ashamed of a proclivity for poetry: try writing a love poem to someone you really don't love, and see how you fidget in your chair. A deeply felt emotion, on the other hand, will guide your hand like a Greek Muse.

But suppose that poetry is foreign to you, or you see your lover (can we still use the archaic but beautifully accurate "beloved"?) every day. Does it make sense to write letters to each other?

It's even better. When you write from a distance, it's too easy to fall back on local trivia and gossip rather than to say something. When a senior editor at Time Magazine decided to "escape" from his wife and from his inflated life-style and flee to Pago Pago, he told the story in the form of an extended letter to his spouse. Hardly a love letter, of course; but really no letter at all, beyond the extensive use of "you" throughout it. This was not because the personal revelations were not there; rather they were the revelations of an onlooker, instead of a participant. The talk was about *me* rather than you. In a true love (or hate, they are waves on the same vibration) letter, the writer is trying to summon *you* up from nowhere, with the pen as his wand. The style of writing is not important; it is "you-talk" rather than "me-talk."

(At cocktail parties, an author uses "book-talk," and a mother uses "baby-talk"—to bring the subject around to one's own field of interest—far too often to be explained by chance. As an observer of this ritual has remarked about herself, "She wants to go to a party and be listened to with the same rapt interest and eye-contact attention women have been extending to men all their lives.")

A lawyer would shudder at the next thought, but at this stage of contract writing we are not as concerned with the law as with the law-like effects of a personal agreement. The thought is this: upon analysis, what one says in a letter is about as binding as anything one is ever likely to do.

How many contracts does the average person sign? Every publishing contract ever written has probably been broken by the author's failure to deliver the manuscript on time. The only other documents I have signed have been mortgages and notes. A businessman signs a contract, in effect, when he agrees in a letter to deliver such and such merchandise for a given price. But for the vast majority of adults, the only serious writing one does is an exchange of letters.

There are two aspects to the love letter as a contract: when does it have legal force, and when does it have "merely" psychological force? As the reader has by now guessed, I would place the "merely" next to "legal force." An agreement to marry might be proved from a series of letters. Passionate protestations of affection in perfumed envelopes—to a third party—are the *piece de resistance* of the divorce courts (or they used to be). An unwillingness to have children has been proved in court by quotations from letters. Yet all of these legal uses of the contents of letters are negative. No matter what one is required to do, by law, in a marriage, a steadfast refusal to do it can only be broken by breaking the marriage. You can lead a horse to water, but you can't make him drink—least of all by shooting him.

What really is worth discussing, therefore, is the psychological force of love letters. To see how immense that is, let's look at a love letter (not one of mine, but a real one), and then, keeping a straight face, run through a quick course in how to write a love letter "that sells!" (Whether you know it or not, the faceless corporation that solicits your subscription to a magazine writes you a love letter.)

> "Dear Mary,
>
> I thought of you last night when I was driving home, and what you said about your new job. I really *do* want to know about what you're doing there—all I meant was I think *you* are more interesting than a silly—pardon me—job. But I'm really glad you like it, because it's part of you and that's where I come in! Whatever happens, do work that *you* want to do, not to please your family or someone unimportant like me. Oh yes, I intend to be important to you later on. I've been pretty mixed up lately when it comes to our future plans. But I'm ready to spring the news to Dad and Mom if you are. I think they know it already. We're out of the hand holding stage, obviously. I guess what I like about you is you want to be sure of all the details before you rush into something. OK. I'm eager. You eager, too? I'll be more eager after a week on the road—as you may gather from my forthcoming missives. I'll call from Chicago if you'll be home Tuesday night. You *will* be, I presume. When we settle down, you can bet I won't be just a "travelling man." Don't believe me? I can take only so much from this company, as you well know. Even the receptionists seem to wince a little when I give them my card, like, "Oh, that again." By the way, forget comparisons with receptionists. Most of them can barely remember a man's name. Beauty just *ain't* skin deep. Hey, what do you see in me, anyway? Don't answer. Just wrap yourself around a good book and take the phone off the hook tonight. Next time, *you* can take a trip and write me a letter. I love yours. But that's only natural, 'cause I love you. Say it again, Sam—only next time, in the *flesh.*
>
> Love, oh yes!
Tom

Now, the analysis. What is Tom *really* saying? How much of it is really indicative of a "love situation?" and where is it psychologically binding?

First, there are tell-tale signs of personal dependence in the writer's self-deprecating (almost nauseating) references to himself: "Someone unimportant like me," or "What do you see in me anyway?" Social scientists have noted that popular song writing thrives on the feeling of inadequacy. In the forties and fifties, love lyrics wallowed in melancholy, self-pity, and submission to fate. "Don't Get Around Much Any More," "Blue Moon," and the ironic, "I Get Along Without You Very Well" typically strike this chord of sweet sadness. Though the letter writer "Tom" expressed these feelings in something less than a poetic way, his emotions are genuine, and the expression of dependence on another person, no matter how poorly worded, is a basic tip-off of love. By means of these informal introductory hints, which are instinctively understood by "Mary," the writer works himself up to actually saying "I love you." By the time he says it, its honesty is established.

Second, the casual mention of job situations—both of them—reveals serious intentions about the future. In this case, both jobs present problems. Implicit in the discussion of working conditions is "Tom's" promise to find a job that will keep him closer to home, with a respectable company, and without ruling out a career for his wife. If he had tried to write contract terms that would specify the same things, he would have been tongue-tied; he has said in an informal way everything that needed to be said.

The particular virtue of the letter form is that it allows otherwise painful or distressing questions to be raised naturally. The casual, almost superficial and unthinking style of this particular letter cannot disguise the intent of the writer nor the seriousness of the issues he is tackling.

It is easy enough to sneer at the rather unsophisticated "patter" of the writer—the gauche attempts at humor ("Say it again, Sam"), the "cute" wordiness ("missives," "ain't"), the hesitant bravado ("in the flesh"). These are signs of an incipient education, not unfamiliar to teachers of Freshman English. An "uneducated" man is likely to write a more direct letter, in basic Anglo-Saxon words. A formal education has the unfortunate tendency to imprison one in a shell of clichés. No matter how bad the style, however, the sentiments come through loud and clear.

If it is true, then, that even the most innocent looking letter can in reality contain the elements of a contract, why not set out specifically to discuss your marriage terms in letter form?

For some people, such an exercise would be self-defeating. Instead of a letter, you might wind up with a dissertation. The essence of a letter is that it is meant to exist for itself alone, and for one person's eyes alone. Knowing that someone is looking over your shoulder and that you are discussing Important Questions might activate all of the defense mechanisms that are ruinous to full disclosure.

What we come back to again is revelation. To reveal oneself thoroughly is the heart of the matter. To reveal oneself *just* to become open with your lover—and not on some pretext of legality or "improvement of communications" or equal rights—is all that counts. As a practical suggestion, therefore, I believe that we can make a distinction between writing letters *intending* them to become a contract, and writing letters for their own sake, with awareness of their psychological value.

Find excuses to write letters. Get out of the postcard, greeting card habit. Free yourself from the illiteracy of clichés by taking more time to think out your letters. Write little notes instead of telephoning or waiting to talk in person. If you are married or living together, and there are no prying eyes around, leave messages on a blackboard or bulletin board. When you give a gift, also give more than a perfunctory greeting. Quote poetry if you don't feel you want to try writing some yourself. Give the things that speak: books, paintings, personal items. Do all of this with the dim awareness in the back of your mind that everything you say can be held against you, that you are writing some unearthly type of contract with yourself as much as with your loved one, but make sure that this remains only a dim awareness. Realize what you're doing, but then just do it.

In short, sign your name as much as you can, but don't put a dotted line under it.

4 Dialogue: the Spoken Contract

When the United States Senate passed its 1972 version of a child-care bill, a sentence was tacked on at the last minute "to meet conservative objections." That bit of wisdom was that the family is the cornerstone of healthy child development.

This is not the first time, of course, that elected officials have thought it necessary to pay lip service to "the family" as a "cornerstone." This cornerstone has been chipped away at, it is claimed, by the liberal divorce laws of Nevada, Idaho, and Arkansas; by the new sexual morality; by communes; and now by child-care centers. The threat of such centers to our conservative society is that they provide an alternative to a mother to being house-bound. Pretty soon, a mother will get the idea that she need not remain married just to care for her children. And this "creeping feminism" could lead eventually to the deterioration of the family—so it is alleged.

When sex education in the schools was first raised as an issue, there was a similar outpouring of lip service to the "primary responsibility" of parents to provide the facts of life.

The point of this introduction is that we continue to rely on public sentiments and pious exhortations long after we recognize them for what they really are: just lip. Most of the present attempts at marriage contracts fall into this category—even though they are in fine legalese and are detailed to the point of being impossibly restrictive. We have observed that love letters are a natural form of contract. We should not overlook the fact that *spoken* contracts are legally binding unless specifically required to be in writing (as is the financial agreement, or antenuptial settlement). Unfortunately, dialogue between a man and a maid seldom covers the problem areas of marriage, and even then often is only lip service.

The plea that I would make here, therefore, is that those in love (whether married already or not) should realize that *talk counts,* and that they should spend a little time thinking about what to talk *about.*

Everyone says dialogue is great: nobody says how to achieve it.

The subjects of good dialogue seem to fall into three categories: the easy, but trivial; the difficult, easily glossed over; and the difficult, "not polite to bring up." When you have trouble putting your thoughts down on paper, the experts say just start writing—anything. The same is true of talking. The sound barrier must be broken, even with trivia.

The dialogue in any good novel is 90% trivia; but it comes easily and it etches a picture with its hundreds of faint strokes. At a football game, to which a girl has gone out of a combined sense of duty and curiosity, a boy might try to show his familiarity with the players and with the course of the play; or, alternatively, he might try to interpret the whole spectacle of cheering for a professional team which has no real claim to his loyalty. Or they both might simply enjoy the fresh air and the feeling of being in a crowd. Whatever the conversation, the accumulation of small insights eventually reveals a full picture of each to the other. So the easy-but-trivial dialogue is not to be dismissed as unimportant. The trick is to get off this level at an early stage.

The difficult subjects, such as sexual relations, children, equal responsibility, careers, alcohol and other drugs, and finances are natural parts of any conversation if they are introduced on the right level—that is, a serious level. Books, magazines, newspapers, movies, and television are perfect openers.

"There's a good article on page 28, Bill."

"The one about adoption? Yeah, I read the first part."

"Well, you missed the point of it then. I think it's fantastic."

"I skimmed it. Something about Chinese kids in an orphanage."

"Bill, why don't you read it again? I think that couple who adopted ought to be on Page One."

"Oh."

"OK. Maybe you don't know it, but we ought to think about adopting . . ."

"Yeah it's a good idea—what!?

In a movie or novel, the chance of one or both parties identifying strongly with one of the characters is a boon to meaningful conversation. The greatest adventure story written or filmed is the search for one's self. The decision of the main character to choose a life-style poses the same question to the reader of viewer: What would he do? What does he want, after all, in life? What do a husband and wife want, when all the immediate pressures of making a living, finding a home, raising children, and taking care of relatives are temporarily forgotten?

It's too easy to walk out of a movie in a numbed state, and say "that was great," and go back to everyday reality as if this ought to be called reality at all. The internal life is the only reality—a message that cries out from every human accomplishment worth noting.

As a practical step, then, I suggest "forced conversation" about shared experiences—on the screen or on the printed page. There is nothing more delightful than arguing an issue or an event, then, intrigued by what the "experts" have to say on the subject, looking up the reviews or critiques. It gives one a great feeling of confidence in the value of his own judgments. Here are some typical questions that can lead to serious discussions, if we only avoid glib answers:

1. Can we live on less money, with fewer possessions, without feeling embarrassed in front of our friends? Do we really have the confidence in ourselves to laugh at the usual social values and pressures? (For 9 out of 10, the honest answer is No.)

2. All right then. Do we al least have some areas where we can go our own way without feeling the critical gaze of our neighbors? For example, can we decline the cocktail party circuit? Can we avoid the siren call of the suburbs? Can we stop going to that expected Sunday morning church service when we do not really believe in its other-worldly value? Can we admit to being old-fashioned about premarital sex or postmarital loyalty? Can we keep friends who are no longer in our "social class?"
3. Can we talk to each other about sex without referring to some bestseller on the subject? Can we say "I love you" out loud and in earnest?
4. Can we handle money without distrust or condescension toward the other party? Can we even talk about who should handle what aspect of finances without wounded pride and guilt?
5. How much time should be spent on any children we might have? Do we use our children to mirror our own differences?

The danger of cold, calculated, enforced conversation is that self-consciousness can make it all just an exercise. A woman who spends all her time with kids during the day naturally wants adult conversation at the end of the day. When she says, "You never talk to me," the killing reply is, "OK—what do you want to talk about?" Humor is the saving grace. If a couple can laugh at this oft-repeated scene, the conversation that follows can warm up very quickly.

The "forbidden" areas of conversation are another matter. Just prior to the flight to divorce, one of the parties is likely to blurt out, "You ought to see a psychiatrist." The challenge is often taken up with the remark, "Let's go together," the implication being that *then* we'll find out who really is bonkers. Another bottomless pit of frustrated conversation is likely to be dug by such remarks as "You have a problem," or "What's wrong with you?" Both questions are ways of disguising the unmentioned problem that may have been causing trouble for years. Is it alcohol? Is it a roving eye? Is it lack of sexual fulfillment? Is it an inability to break out of the mold of a parent's character? Is it resentment over lack of a satisfying career? Is it jealousy over what the other party seems to be achieving or enjoying? Sometimes, you and you alone can answer these questions. Sometimes, only a psychiatrist can.

The difference is in *how early in life* you ask them.

5 the Secret Contract

The strongest bond between two people, the basic understanding, the deepest commitment, the finest balance, and the most precarious involvement is the bond of sexual closeness. It would not be important to repeat and emphasize this pre-eminent fact except for the common misunderstanding that sex is, and only is, sexual intercourse. When the "question man" asks the man or woman in the street if sex is over-emphasized in our society, many people answer "yes" because by "sex" they mean copulation and only that. Conversely, those who answer "no" usually do so for the same reason. Few "love manuals" or newspaper columns on sex offer more than advice on bedroom athletics.

The "secret contract" I refer to in this chapter is sex in its broadest implications. And the best I can come to expressing what this involves is by the phrase "sexual closeness." In this sense, sex is all important.

I am sexually "close" to my mother and father, to my children, to people around me at work, and to my wife. The *degree* of closeness is everything. Because I am (or should be) irrevocably close to my wife, and she to me, I can abandon myself to her in my most personal, even secret, feelings, needs, desires. I can expose myself mentally and physically to a doctor, but never in the totally personal way that I reveal myself in all my glaring humanity to my beloved. When I say "I," I mean "all of us," and when I say "can," I mean "should."

The implications of this simple truth are more alarming than one might imagine at first sight. To start with, we do not need a Simone de Beauvoir to reassure us (but it helps) that "sex" is possible and even urgent after fifty or sixty years of age. It is self-evident when you take "sex" in its fullest meaning. Every human being in being human stands in a sexual relationship with someone else. And if by "sex" one specifically means "doing it," then the question becomes one of mere muscular capability, of physics. To have sexual intercourse without having sexual *closeness* in attitude, feeling, awareness, and "reckless abandon" is to forever eat nothing more than the cherry off the sundae. (One must admit that metaphors cannot adequately express the implications of "loveless" intercourse.)

It helps, also, to speak in terms of closeness rather than "love." In the above example, it is commonplace to say that sex without love is empty. A woman particularly senses the inner betrayal in a crass physical relationship devoid of personal attachment—which is perhaps why a man is thought of as having a "mistress" while a woman has a "lover." To avoid the implications of such broad terms as "love," therefore, it is often helpful to talk merely of personal *closeness*—whether that closeness be casual friendship or emotional stupefaction.

What is of greatest concern here, after this brief clarification of terms, is that what I call the secret ritual of sex is a contract of inestimable worth; and that such a contract can be enlarged and enfused with unexpected life by recognizing its contractual possibilities. In short, you'll make a better "fit" in the life of your mate once you realize how much sex is involved in everything you think and do.

A popular song of some years back put it very simply:

> Oh how we danced
> On the night we were wed;
> We vowed our true love
> Though a word wasn't said.

From the point of view I am advocating here, you can vow your true love as much in making a peanut butter sandwich as in dancing on your wedding night. There are two aspects to this point of view: first, to convince you that this is not just a romantic will of the wisp; second, to show how practical steps can be taken to make a real contract out of a "mere" ritual.

The "secrecy" of sex gives a clue to its vitality and pervasiveness in everyone's life. What is secret is really what is *shared*, at its highest level, between *two* people. The cynic says that the perfect newspaper headline is "Scientist Claims Black is White." We are fascinated by a paradox, especially if it originates from an authority figure (a scientist today, or a cleric yesterday). The cynic is only partly right; what most fascinates a reader is something that speaks to him as a person. The perfect newspaper headline is more likely something on the order of "Lovers Ignore Family, Wealth, Success; Seek Only Each Other." (Perhaps this is not too different from the cynic's headline.)

Paradox though it may seem, it is the *secrecy* of sexual commitment which makes sex so universally attractive, not to say compelling. The following is a very "unromantic" list of the forms of sexual commitment that occur every day in a normal relationship.

1. *Physical Oddities.* Husband and wife cannot long hide from each other certain peculiarities of their bodies that would otherwise not interest or bother a casual acquaintance. The imperfection of the human body in the most glorious athlete or beauty queen is quickly made obvious after a few months of cohabitation. Far from a cause for shame or disgust, however, these peculiarities are part of the very stuff of "closeness." To be able to doff the protective armor of supports and "glamorizing" clothes is the first step to sharing one's humanity with another person. The columnists preach a different tract. They would advise you that "to keep romance alive" you should perpetuate the illusion of Grecian perfection in limb and visage. Perhaps this is true *when you cease being secret,* when you put your best foot forward to the outside world. And, of course, honesty in appearance is no license to become a slob. Steering between both extremes, the couple that can live with each

other's physical frailties, and even make something out of them, is the couple that is on the right track.

As in most areas of earthly wisdom, physical factors must be considered first, and are usually at the bottom of socalled "higher" emotions and aspirations.

One of the most endearing terms I have heard applied to a wife of many years, by a sensitive and loving husband, is "Fatty." In one paradoxically apropos word he has touched lightly on a shared concern over a slight weight "problem," simultaneously taking the sting out of the thought yet reminding her that the frailty is there, laughing at himself for being so concerned over a point that only women are supposed to be concerned with, pushing his honesty with her to the normal limits that any couple could sustain on a touchy subject, and leaving himself wide open, on purpose, to a similar jab at his own baldness or slowness or whatever. Fanciful? I don't think so. The impact of a nickname is generated from a hundred shared feelings, so subtle and so intimate (which is to say secret), that the only difficulty in recognizing them is in analyzing something that disappears under analysis. If the name fits, both will know why without saying.

2. *Habits.* A second area of personal interrelationship in which husband and wife exhibit sexual closeness is patterned behavior—that is, instinctual or learned habits. A surprising fact about human response surfaces here. Habits which are annoying, even disgusting to two people who are *not* sexually close are magically transformed into bonds of love or at least friendship between two people who are fired with a sexual attraction. Psychologists consistently overlook the possibility of such a transformation. It does not fit into the normal pattern of behavior; it seems to credit mystical powers to "love." Is it more than poetic hallucination? Consider the evidence of everyday life.

In an office or a factory or a school, coworkers drive each other to extreme anguish over such trivial-sounding complaints as a nasal twang of speech, sloppy handwriting, pecuniousness, a fondness for sweets, overdressing, body odor, or excessive use of perfume, dirty fingernails, consistent tardiness, scratching, or a nervous cough. One of the great saints of Christian tradition, Theresa of Liseaux, is said to have had a more profound influence on the missionary work of the church than a hundred globetrotting clerics; yet she never left her convent. And in her own personal development she relates that one of her greatest hurdles was to learn to tolerate a fellow nun who had an annoying way of fingering her beads! The best of friends can put up with each other's mannerisms for only short lengths of time. The familiarity that "breeds contempt" among business associates or coworkers is pleasantly avoided by distractions of drink, sports, or a third party. How then is it possible for husband and wife to tolerate, even indulge, each other's peculiarities of behavior for ten or twenty years?

It is my contention that those who say it is just not possible, that this is the basic argument for short-term unions, for mistresses, or for living together but in mental twin beds, have already missed the point of married love. Indeed, it is *not* possible for mere friends to live with each other's mannerisms for even a few months. The alternative explanation is *not* that married couples somehow learn the tolerance of a St. Theresa, but that their love actually exerts a transformation of annoyances into fascination (for want of a better name). A mystical theory? Yes.

Songwriters have a way of hinting all around this central point. "Oh, how the ghost of you clings, these foolish things remind me of you." The things that get in one man's hair are the very same that get under another man's skin—in a favorable way—and "you can't take that away from me."

A messy pipe that would repel a housekeeper becomes a part of the life of a happy wife. Fussiness in dressing that would distract a father or son cements the affection of a husband. An attachment to a boat or an antique automobile or a stamp collection is no longer some sexual symbol of inadequacy, but just one tangible part of a whole person which a wife can share as part of her knowledge of her husband.

The sequence in this "magical" transformation is cyclical. Complete honesty, self abandon of oneself to another, leads to a kind of sexual closeness. This closeness assimilates the idiosyncrasies of one partner to the other, in such a way that the "faults" of one become the "faults" of the other. Thus peculiarities of behavior, that in themselves are burrs, become flowers. And in turn this transformation of annoyances into sources of attachment opens further doors of personal honesty.

This attempt at a psychological explanation of the process of love is, of course, barely rational. One is inclined to say "Leave it to poets, songwriters, and other fools." But understand me: I propose all of this not as a theory but as a way of re-evaluating one's behavior, as a call to action. Because it is merely rhetoric does not mean it is not effective.

So far I have cited physical oddities and habits of behavior as examples of areas of *sexual closeness*. It is worth pausing here to consider why these mundane matters are properly called "sexual" in any sense of the word—for this is my central argument, that these things are of the essence of sexuality. Just because they are examples of human honesty, of total exposure of two people to each other, why do I insist on calling them sexual? Isn't the common usage of the term confined to some connection with sexual intercourse?

One could answer in traditional psychological terms. The love of a father and daughter as well as the conflict of a father and son are freely referred to as sexual. In my opinion, too much is borrowed *literally* from the Oedipus myth to explain a sexual connection in these textbook cases. As sweeping and rudimentary as it is as a theory—and this is its finest recommendation—the desire of a son to marry his mother is more difficult to swallow than the events it is designed to explain. It is less dramatic, but more helpful, to think in terms of "closeness." Mother and child have always been closer to each other physically and emotionally in the course of a civilization in which father is a warrior and a worker, an artisan or politician. At some point the awareness that the other sex is, let us say, *complementary* to one's own sex dawns on the young child. This feeling need not be explained further than that it is obviously based on some remote promise of reproduction. That the promise may never be realized is of no concern. The result is the same—or, as a cynic might say, the threat is stronger than the execution.

To summarize: the closeness of two people becomes "sexual" by the mere biological possibility of copulation. The possibility may be purely residual, with no real potential at all—as in the case of the extreme aged. Yet their closeness is sexual in its biological derivation. In a "sexually active" couple in the conventional sense, intercourse is like a votive lamp that radiates its eternal promise in the slightest physical contact. But this is not to say that a more sedate couple is not equally infused with sexual delight in each other's presence. In an almost perversely extreme case, the flame of affection burned more fiercely between the castrated Abelard and the cloistered Heloise than in any recorded romance of their contemporaries.

The culmination of sexuality is, in fact, usually less than (or more than) physical even in the very act of intercourse. In our era of the "liberated" press, in which an inquiring photographer or a radio talk show can ask and say just about anything except the actual four-letter word, one small benefit is that we are actually learning how people think and act without the inhibiting mediation of a Kinsey Report or a Dr. Reuben. For example, a recent man in the street survey established (at least among the few who were willing to publish their views under their pictures) that people like to laugh while "doing it"—sometime. I take this as a healthy attitude—laughter being the only sure-fire indication intelligence. At the very least this attitude demolishes the idolators of physical prowess as the be-all and end-all of love-making. These mechanics—from Masters and Johnson to Jacqueline Suzanne—have done more to trigger false expectations and arouse unfounded anxieties than all of the Victorian moralists and Irish pastors in half a century of scolding. "Lovemaking" and "having sex" are phrases that are minimally descriptive; the sex manuals have managed to make their product match the poverty of these descriptions.

To return to the point: intercourse is a joining of far more than penis and vagina or any other parts of the body. At best it is a total abandon of one person to another, and vice versa—emotions, mind, dreams. At its worst, it is a physical experiment, but even then between two whole persons and not between two machines.

The third way, then, of how two people can become sexually close to each other is emotionally.

3. *Emotional Needs.* The hug at the airport, the swinging arm in arm down the street, the shoulder rub, the touching of knees under the table, the grin that jumps from eye to eye all approach the level of "love-making" but never require it for the fullest enjoyment. They are ends in themselves. They are the stuff of courtship, of perpetual seeking for a richer experience. And in the seeking comes the realization.

Because the actual courtship is over and the bargain made, any further efforts in this direction are often thought of either as regressive behavior, or an awkward attempt to stay young (as in the man who thinks it amorous to refer to his wife as his "bride"), or worse, as a *real* courtship or reconciliation. As a Russian chess master is fond of saying, "Why so difficult?" Why can't we take this "continuing courtship" simply as fun in itself—and hence a simple renewal of the marriage contract? This is the nub of the matter: every expression of sexual closeness reaffirms "we are one."

The New Testament description of marriage is not taken in its full literal sense—and it *should* be: for this a man shall leave his father and mother and cleave to his wife, and they shall become one flesh. In no deep, mystical sense, husband and wife inhabit each other's bodies, as they do their emotions.

Our natural impulse, especially in 20th century America, is to accept this analysis as a flight of fancy, a turgid muddling of a rather mundane subject, namely, how to get along with the opposite sex in or out of marriage. The "realists" of American journalism, from H. L. Mencken to Charles McCabe, espouse a barroom wisdom in which the American husband makes a bargain early in life to keep emotions from interfering with the real rewards of living—such as a beer on a hot day, the recognition of a few peers as belonging to a way of life, the machismo of "making it" in the workaday world, and the occasional luxury of a point of view. In this world, love is a temporary blindness, a gift for the young who have not yet learned the realities of life; sex is a problem, an explosive commodity at once to be feared, guarded against, and sought after in the dark of night. The American observer protects himself from sexual commitment in humor. McCabe reports that the distilled wisdom of the great American hero, the bartender, is that tall girls are appreciative and short girls are Napoleons. This knowledge quite naturally makes more sense to the American male than volumes on affairs of the heart. All I ask here is that a passing thought be given to the most powerful force in one's being—the emotions—when we ask the question "What does it mean to be married to someone?"

The emotions are the final bond that weld two people into one—or, better, that dissolve them into one. This is a contract, which, once entered into, keeps on writing itself—like the printout from a wire service teletype.

All of the foregoing theory about the nature of sexual *closeness* is a preliminary for what I believe are the essentials of a sexual contract—the "secret ritual." First, recognize it as ritual, but don't for a minute suspect that ritual is some sort of unreality—some formality that hides the way things really are. Ritual is behavior that shapes our hearts. Second, recognize the pervasiveness of sex in our lives. Third, recognize the evidence of how sex transforms the ordinary or the objectionable into the special and the satisfying. Fourth, put all of this in the framework of a contract and see what practical "leaps forward" are possible. Finally, take a hard, cold look at the illusory "contracts" that are offered in the current literature by psychologists, marriage counselors, advice to the lovelorn columnists, and writers of best-seller fiction.

The first requisite of "the secret contract," as of any contract, is the exclusion of all others from the agreement and even from the terms of the agreement. In the grotesque love affair in the film, "Diary of a Mad Housewife," the embryo mistress suggests that her lover come to a party being prepared by her husband. Her lover devastates her with his retort, to the effect, "So we'll play the only-you-and-I-know game and walk around like we're invisible!" The remark is cruel precisely because it hits at the heart of the woman's desire for a private compact, the desire to live in one's own world oblivious to all else, secure in the knowledge that one and only one other human being is "in" on her affair. Such a feeling is not confined to sexual encounters, but it seems paramount to a love affair that is destined to be more than an experiment.

The first piece of practical advice, then, is to exclude

neighbors, friends, and relatives from sharing the slightest intimacy of your lover and you. The love stories that haven't been told, I am sure, are the great unheard melodies of all time. I would even go so far as to advise that public or semi-public displays of intimacy be discouraged—when they are more than just natural ebullience. It would seem to me that communal living is the severest test of the human psyche to maintain a one-to-one contract. The suggestion made from time to time by a "free thinking" counselor that parents should make love in front of their children strikes me as being equally opposed to the basic need of "secrecy." Because sex is good does not mean it should be openly observed. The real tawdriness of "sex shows" is not their evil consequences nor their violation of public decency, but their *joylessness*—a joylessness that comes from the surrender of the performers' privacy, which is to say their persons.

Whether or not it is somehow in the "nature of man" that *secrecy* between two people gives them a special unity, I do not know. Perhaps it is only pressing at this moment in history because of the constant threats and inducements to yield to the scrutiny of society. As a practical matter, however, there is little question but that sexual closeness begins with those little one-to-one secrets that we cultivate first as small children, later as sons and daughters, finally as unabashed lovers.

A sexual contract is written in the actions that signify surrender of oneself to another. It is truly meaningless to take pen in hand and to promise sexual performance so many times a week. Sex so permeates a person's whole being that it would be equally ridiculous to promise in writing that you would be a good person so many times a week. At every level of human awareness, one must resist the suggestion that behavior can be counted by numbers, or that individual actions all added together make up a person. For centuries we have labored in the belief that there are such things as sins, mortal and venial—individual actions we perform which, when totalled, add up to a sinful person. But there is only sin (singular) and there is only evil; and a man is sinful or he isn't to some *degree.* In the same way a man is sexually close to his partner or he is not; but his merit or fault is not in "how many times" he does something.

The secret is not to hold back the "surrender" of oneself—even though our particular culture encourages us to remain aloof, to "maintain our identity" in front of even our lover. The paradox of sexual closeness, as we have alluded to already, is that our identity grows by being submerged in another, that what we "give up" becomes stronger, that our faults become virtues—not in some sort of misery-loves-company melting pot, but in the shared humanity of another.

In the old days we were admonished by our elders and moral counselors that sexual contact had a place and time, and that we should shut our minds to any pleasure we there experienced, outside that place and time. We should not "dwell on" the glories of the bedchamber, we were told, nor look forward to them with anything resembling eager anticipation. In this fractionated world, it was presumed that men (and sometimes even women) could don their animal masks at the appointed hour, "satisfy" themselves, then return to the Victorian world like some Dr. Jekyll. The revels of Mr. Hyde were to be a necessary evil, a concession to a lower nature.

How little did these latter-day Augustinians realize the depth and elasticity of the human personality! Little did they realize that a woman can (and perhaps must) be at one and the same time a saucy mistress, a gentlewoman, a protective mother, and a shrewd businesswoman. Or that a man could change from a leering satyr to a proper gentleman kissing his wife goodbye at the train station, in the space of a few hours. What we have learned about ourselves as human beings (in spite of Freud) is that we do not have to worry about being dominated by unconscious feelings of guilt, by recriminations, by stifled emotions or repressed desires. We can throw ourselves recklessly to another human being, and still earn that person's respect. In fact, we only grow as persons by learning to forget about our own growth and about deliberate ways to achieve it.

In passing, it is worth noting here that it is this requisite of sexual "generosity" which argues most strongly for fidelity in marriage and for perseverence in fidelity. It is difficult to see how a person can give himself fully to more than one person at a time, or that once having given himself he can lightly take himself back. But this is a whole subject in itself, discussed in another context in the Epilogue.

We can turn more of our actions in the direction of forming a "sexual contract" simply by doing consciously less for ourselves and more for our beloved. We *can* learn to want more for the other, less for ourselves. We can start by deciding this does not diminish our own personality. We can then free ourselves of the bonds we unconsciously create by our fortress-like protection of our own psyche. When we stop worrying about how we can defend ourselves, what we should have said or should have done, how we can react to the other's faults or supposed threat to us, then we will be free to grow as our own nature requires.

The final paradox is that a sexual contract—secured by the total exposure of two persons to each other—is the only source of sexual "liberation." Such a liberation is complete; it is not merely a demand by a woman for sexual gratification nor an escape by a man from loyalty to a single woman. It is complete in the sense that it encompasses bodily differences, behavior, emotions, and not just actual intercourse. Such a liberation is the freedom of self-knowledge; only here is is the self-knowledge of two people of each other. It is only the person who is not secure in that self-knowledge who is always looking, hoping, for an "adventure," who always feels he is missing out on something, or who simply equates living with diversion, so out of touch with a real life he is.

I do not pretend to have personally acted out the role of liberated, dedicated, self-denying spouse which I have described in idealistic terms in this chapter. I am only an observer; perhaps the best observer is the non-participant. We all think we know the right thing to do—the problem is doing it. The total commitment of a sexual compact, *I know* is the finest contract of all. It requires all of the prescriptions mentioned in this chapter—to some degree. And it will result in a marriage liberated to the capacity of each partner to liberate himself and herself, and to "find" themselves in each other.

6 the Rites of Love

When a mass wedding ceremony for several thousand "common law" couples was recently celebrated in Mexico City, the value of ritual was given its most resounding public demonstration within memory. Not even for the marriage of a Queen have the wedding bells rung out so triumphantly!

Yet ritual has always been tinged with superstition in the minds of "practical" Americans. The full force of ritual, however, has never really been challenged as it occurs in the daily life of everyone of us. It is not just habit that causes us to have that customary cup of coffee with the morning paper, to greet fellow bus riders with the ceremonial "How are you?" and to walk a certain well-defined path to the office, avoiding some streets and preferring others. Everything we do, the psychologists are quick to remind us, is flavored with meaning. The way we hold a cigarette, the ties we wear, the music we listen to—all have significance if we only knew it or cared to analyze it.

Probably the greatest single ritual act of modern America is the trek to the professional football game on Sunday afternoon. The pageantry of the medieval church could not rival the color, the conviviality, nor the abstract symbolism of the pro game. The "visiting" and the "home" teams are protagonists in an earthy morality play—a drama acted out, as only real life can direct, by fretting coaches, Napoleonic quarterbacks, villains turned heroes, goalline stands, the bitterness and frustration of defeated favorites, the nobility of underdogs. There is no dearth of physical dexterity, of course; but I suggest that of all the theories attempting to explain our fascination with sporting events on a coliseum scale, including sublimation of aggressions, identification with our day dream idols, and the love of crowds and parades, the most satisfactory is the simple idea of drama and its rituals.

It is worth thinking about the impact of ritual in our non-religious, non-emotional moments simply because it explains why we succeed in important areas of our lives and what we can do to improve that success. Ritual, in my meaning, is not window dressing: it is substance. The performing of a rite is neither a magical incantation nor an empty gesture. It is something worthwhile in itself, because it creates attitudes and values that otherwise would not come to life.

A few examples. A parade of war veterans, with its banners and publicity, states a point of view. More important than the public point of view is the private impact of solidarity which the parade leaves on its immediate audience. A handful of earth is strewn into a grave at a formal funeral ceremony, saying more than a full-dress sermon at the Requiem Mass. Roses arrive at the door to say "I love you" in a special way, even though the ritual of sending flowers has become so automatic it is almost expected.

This last fact in itself is enough to hint that ritual is worthwhile for its own sake. No matter how expected, many ritual acts preserve their social values without the slightest implication that overuse would lead to absurdity. Thus the religious minded are inspired by ceremonies that seem to grow in efficacy with mere repetition. For others, ceremonial rites quickly grow irksome and, as I said at the beginning, superstitious.

The rites of love are part of the total tradition of ritual in our society. The points I wish to make here are that these rites are, first, valuable in themselves and, second, essential parts of a marriage contract, whether we recognize it or not.

In all the standard treatises on marriage rites, from Edward

Westermarck to Bruno Bettelheim, there is an endless recitation of the customs of ancient people, medieval nomads, and modern "savages" in the area of sex and marriage. An interesting feature of these tiresome accounts is that half of the evidence supports one thesis, and half of the evidence supports an opposite thesis. "... In Russia the bridegroom formerly used to beat the bride on the head with the bootleg to show that she was now in his power and had to obey him; but among the Slovenes the bride nowadays beats the bridegroom with the bootleg, as if to make him understand that she is not always going to pull off his boots," is one typical bit of trivia collected by Westermarck. Bettelheim and the more "modern" sociologists lean heavily on Freudian and anti-Freudian analysis. Every gesture, to the average reader, would seem to bear on fear of castration, on unconscious remembrance of circumcision, or on fertility rites. Two basic assumptions of contemporary psychologists/sociologists, which this whole book challenges, are (1) that ritual has a meaning only as an unenlightened substitute for rationality, and (2) that the similarity of certain ritual forms means that ritual is a meaningless habit.

Without being explicit, sociologists have implied that only primitive societies "needed" the support of ritual decorations and exercises. Bettelheim begins his "Introitus" to *Symbolic Wounds* (Thomas and Hudson, 1955) with a reference to the religious beliefs and rituals that "were probably the first inventions of the human mind once it ceased to be occupied solely with physical survival." "Our curiosity led us," he says, "to wonder ... what were the emotional needs they were meant to satisfy." At the start, therefore, it is assumed that ritual (and religious beliefs, to boot) were some sort of excess baggage in mankind's development, a coat that could be thrown off when the winds of emotion raged less violently. Then, when it appeared that rituals and beliefs continued to be strong in Western vivilization, these were shown to be only parallels to the old *initation* rites of "Preliterate" society, by which a youth was admitted to adulthood. Because these rituals have some points of comparison (Bettelheim sees all of the sacraments of the Catholic Church, except extreme unction, as variants of initiation rites), the second assumption is that somehow they are less meaningful. For example, if many ancient religions and societies revered a maternal deity, the assumption is that a doctrine of a "Mother of God" in Christian religions is weakened—because it is only another manifestation of a basic human tendency to yearn for a mother. G. K. Chesterton has incisively dealt with this modern fable as "lack of proof because of too much evidence."

What we must consciously resist is the easy rationalization that what everybody tends to do must be the result of mere habit or reflex. This is the cynic's view of love. Because the adolescent "mooning" of many young people is so prevalent, the cynic says it must be just a "stage" through which one passes without really analyzing what he or she is getting into. On the contrary, I think it is more reasonable to take what people do as being a natural part of their makeup. When a man and a maid fall in love, it is not a slackening of their rational behavior, but a completion of their *humanness.*

Yet we are bombarded daily by interpretations of man's (and woman's) simplest and most natural acts as something that had to be culturally "learned." Margaret Mead has gone so far as to call human fatherhood a "social invention." When all of the digressions into the life styles of the Manus or the Mundugumors or Usiai or other obscure peoples are done with, what it comes down to is that anthropologists claim they have no evidence that fathers would "nurture" their children and wives unless they were *taught* to. The question of who nurtures whom is becoming more tightly drawn in the 1970's than in the 1950's of Miss Mead's *Male and Female.* It seems absurd to me to base a theory for something on the lack of evidence to the contrary, when the opportunity for such evidence simply did not exist. Perhaps we will see in our lifetimes what "nurturing" really means, outside of who provides food and shelter.

But for a minute can we forget that there are certain tribes in Africa which perform a ritual chase of the bride, that the engaged aborigines of Australia (some of them, some of the time) draw each other's blood before marriage, or that some American Indian betrothed would lie together without consumating the marriage for several months after the cremony? What happened and still happens in huts is not as pertinent as what happens in pent houses. Let's consider the love rites of 20th century Americans, and how their rituals before, during, and after marriage are a lesson to the rest of us. Our common experience of ritual is that it is, in all its forms, at the same time a seizing and a letting go. It is a shelter and free rain. The wedding ceremony itself, for example, allows pent-up feelings of exuberance, tenderness, or spirituality to be released. The same ceremony focuses the aspirations and desires of the betrothed, in a sense restricting them. What is most impressive in the lives of most young people, however, is the *liberating* quality of the wedding rites.

For most young married people, the wedding ceremony is truly the "initiation" ceremony so dear to the anthropologists. It is the open door to full adulthood: the breaking of all links with parental authority, the invitation to go out and conquer the wide world on your own. And it is the ceremony which conveys this meaning to its fullest. The assembly of friends and relatives is no mere curious crowd: *it is the hand of the community raised in blessing.*

When a famous actress recently announced she would be married to an equally famous "radical," reporters questioned her first as to why the couple would require a wedding ceremony at all. I don't know her answer, but the reporters had already assumed too much about those who opt for alternate life styles in our society. Why should we assume that the ceremony of marriage is any less desired in a commune than on the Main Line? Let's look at the customs of homo sapiens re wedding rites in 20th century America.

In "middle America," we are likely to see ceremonies based on cultural affinities of first or second generation citizens. The Polish, Irish, German, and Italian communities in the Midwest and East are strongly influenced by family ties and by the preservation of cultural values in a marriage. Therefore the ceremony itself tends to become a series of interrelated announcements, pilgrimages to the bride's home town, renewed familiarity between relatives, polite sparring with relatives of the bridegroom, grandiose yet highly traditional church rituals, with the real culmination not in the departure of the bride and groom on their honeymoon but in the festivities of the reception. There is as it should be, in my opinion: the ritual has allowed both the couple *and* all the relatives to "seize" and "let go."

More formal and sedate ceremonies involve the same elements, yet they meet different psychological needs of parents and children raised in a different culture. Though we smile at the formality of an afternoon champagne reception on the manicured lawn of a Long Island estate, we know it is as satisfying to all the requirements of hosts and guests as is a juke-box, beer-keg dance on Chicago's South Side. Ritual is so strong that beer at a reception for many is unthinkable.

Because neither form of celebration seems to benefit the married couple, it seems natural enough to wonder why these "excuses for a party" cannot be done away with and instead all the "wasted" money spent for a better purpose. Engagement rings and even wedding rings seem equally open to criticism. The whole convention would seem to have been invented by merchants—as the retailers have taken over Christmas as promotion and the morticians have undertaken death as a holiday from reason.

In my view, the ceremonies surrounding a wedding are the greatest justification for a "party" in one's lifetime. Engagement rings and even wedding rings I can put aside, but not the human contact of the "marriage moment." All human intercourse has some justification; but this is the moment when two people have decided to become "one flesh." It is a moment of truth if none other ever comes in one's lifetime. In this the anthropologists agree: the promise of a one-to-one relationship exists at the beginning of most marriages. I cannot agree with the odd world of Dr. David Reuben, in which "from the steaming jungles of Africa to the frozen polar wastelands, Mommy, Daddy, and Baby have stood united against the threats of Nature and civilization." In the steaming jungles and polar wastelands are the real *exceptions* to marriage as we know it; and the nuclear family is not at all at odds with Nature and civilization. Just the reverse: because marriage is so deeply rooted in our civilization and (as the Epilogue may show in greater detail) in *Nature,* the wedding ceremony takes on an importance far above anything else in life. For most of us, it is the *signal of adulthood.*

I sense that most modern married couples recognize this as a fact, and do not lean on the bygone delusion that marriage is a mere bargain of convenience. Sociologists are as far behind the advancing consciousness of adults as a weekly newspaper is behind the stock market. Recently a West Coast psychologist announced he had been conducting an experiment to remedy sexual problems of impotency in males, involving the use of "surrogate" mating partners to overcome the blocks and boredom that their wives were apparently not able to counter. Asked if this were not just another form of prostitution, since prostitutes were used successfully in the experiments, the doctor replied that American wives were generally prostitutes anyway—they received security instead of money for their services. In the absence of any evidence for such a sweeping view, shared, by the way, by many women's lib advocates, I think it is better to look for more in a marriage than such a shallow bargain. The facts speak otherwise.

Marriage is even less than a bargain, of course, to many observers. With all the ritual purged away, marriage is to many the *absence of discomfort.* Evelyn Keyes, minor film actress of the late '40's, has achieved this happy state as the eighth wife of Artie Shaw. In a recent newspaper interview, she said, "Do I believe in marriage? Absolutely not. It belongs to another era. Falling in love, that silly thing, I haven't thought in those terms for years, is the worst reason there is to get married." Speaking of Artie, she continues, "After a long time, it becomes unseemly not to stay together. He is my best friend and I trust him never to harm me in any way." Artie agrees, "You marry somebody who says 'The man I love' all day—forget it! . . . I'm very concerned about her. Is that love? I don't know what the word means."

Newspaper accounts are notoriously incomplete on such a personal subject — especially when the person interviewed is trying to make "good copy." Yet the attitude expressed by the Shaws is widespread. All we have to do is to get down to the "business of living," running from love as if it were a UFO. Can we afford to be as aloof, unemotional, and calculating as this other ideal of behavior would indicate?

I come back again to the central idea that ritual *creates* value, one great value being love. If proof were needed of this thesis, consider the studies done in the psychology of friendship. Drs. Ellen Berscheid and Elaine Walster showed in 1972 that physical attractiveness is a disproportionate measure of good character traits: we admire people who "look good." In spite of all the philosophical injunctions to look deeper than at "skin deep" beauty, we unconsciously recognize physical attractiveness as a ritual signifying sensitivity, kindness, modesty, and a host of other noble attributes.

Another index of the importance of ritual in our behavior is the recent movement in favor of taking the "sexist" role out of child rearing. Sociologist Jean Lipman Blumen has documented in scientific terms what women have suspected for years: women's life roles are shaped at an early age by the toys she receives, the example she gets from her father, and the whole cultural impact of a male-dominated society. The income and education of the parents, surprisingly, does not influence her as much as the things in her infant life. The questionnaire used in this study in itself has a ritualistic effect: it caused many respondents to re-examine their life style for the first time.

My argument is that the substance of the marriage contract has not really changed at all: the ritual has changed. And that change is having a profound effect on legal aspects of marriage.

The change in ritual is toward equality of both partners. That change is evident in changing marriage ceremonies and changing life styles. The change has been brought about without the adoption of the women's equality initiatives or other legal proposals currently in the wind. For example, family law has changed in the interpretation of courts to the point where alimony is no longer a life long proposition and child custody is no longer a female prerogative. Louis Nizer argues that because divorced women regardless of age or number of children have a better chance of marriage than single women, and because 94% of all divorced or widowed women are employed, the need for alimony has diminished, and courts have so recognized. What the courts really have recognized is a changing sense of responsibility—for women have been as economically well off for at least thirty years as they are now. Alimony is now to be called "maintenance," and may apply to the husband as well as to the wife. The obligation to support children is joint—not merely that of the father. In 1972 the University of California inaugurated the first course of its kind under its Extension program on the subject of "do-it-yourself" law, and most of it was concerned with the fact that wives should learn about the changing laws on dissolution of marriage. What is happening is that egalitarianism, the lawyer's word for equality, is hitting the law as it has already hit the *ritual* of marriage.

As the chapter heading indicates, the ritual of marriage is not as powerful as the rites of love. I have assumed that love finds its most natural resting place in marriage, but the difference remains. What do I mean by the "rites of love" - in or out of marriage?

The great danger in examining the rites of love is that we automatically tend to invest meaning into the ritual, and thereby destroy it. It is one thing to consciously practice ritual; it is another to try to elevate ritual to something which it is not.

A good example of the misuse of ritual, in my opinion, is the attempt to extract meaning out of religious ceremonies. It is natural enough, in translating Latin to English in the Catholic Mass, to try to make every phrase count. Thus the linquists ponder over the exact meaning of a certain word, with the result that a dramatic King James Bible phrase becomes a twentieth century newspaper account. Liturgy is supposed to become more "meaningful," and so it drops all pretense at emotional import. It is almost as if the theologians feared emotional involvement because of the anticipated criticisms of the "scientific community." Having to retreat to the vernacular, they found safety in the vulgar.

Any ritual, no matter how noble in sentiment or its trappings, becomes empty when a search is made for its "meaning." The Star Spangled Banner has impact only as an empty lyric. Start thinking about it and the history it protrays, and it is nothing. Start rewriting the traditional wedding ceremony, eliminating all the "impossible" promises and substituting more "reasonable" terms, and you will wind up with another boring recitation. We know that many of the "great men" revered in Westminster Abbey were minor criminals in their own day—yet we mark their tombs with grandise statements. A whole nation pays tribute in statues and in words to a man who brought the ravages of war more fiercely to Europe than any man before him—Napoleon. We cannot look too deeply or we will suffer a loss to our humanity.

The first point, then, is thats the rites of love, generally symbolized in the wedding ceremony, are worthwhile and worth cultivating just for themselves and not for their exact significance.

The second point is that the rites of love go on endlessly in the life of a marriage—in many different forms. Inventive couples devise their own secret rituals; others follow pattern dictated by their upbringing. Is it really so? Consider these examples:

A couple I know have created names for each other - "Bear" and "hot stuff." Without knowing the couple, the names are ridiculous. But they happen to have fit something individual in each of them, and they know it. Those are not nicknames except to each other. But each use of the names recalls, however faintly, some shared moment or insight.

Another couple has made a fetish, if that is the appropriate word, out of taking showers together after making love. I say a "fetish" because the shower can occasionally become a substi- for the after glow of intercourse even when intercourse did not occur, for one reason or another! This couple has invested such value in the commonplace that the commonplace gives value.

Most couples have set times for various activities. The times may be seasonal: the visiting of relatives in the Summer, the routine of college football games and class reunions in the Fall. Or the times may be daily: a midmorning phone call to discuss what couldn't be discussed at breakfast, a pre-dinner cocktail together (not quite the same as the habitual cocktail hour, together or not), or a late night reading of the day's paper after the kids are in bed. Finally, the set times may be almost momentary. Conversation between husband and wife (and between other lovers) usually has a rhythm of its own, dictated by past shared conversations. Perhaps it is not out of place to mention a few examples, since we are all too close to our own behavior to be able to see it for what it is.

Built into the most trivial sounding conversation are all the nuances of experiences shared by two speakers. It is often impossible for a man to say "I love you," even if he knows that is exactly what his partner wants to hear, if he has said "I love you" in a different, more emotional, context before. Why? Because he has an innate sense of a violation of a ritual. A man (or a woman) cannot use the same "I love you," of an emotional moment, at a company dance. The meaning is the same; the ritual is not.

Every family builds its own pattern of ritual just as surely as the medieval church established its rites. Certain things are done at certain times—the most important being the observance of each person's individuality—man, woman, or child. Children are given time to speak at the "adult table." Adults are given time to be alone between the clearing of the dinner dishes and the putting of the kids to bed. One couple I know has built a bathtub in their backyard for joint bathing; another has pegged its life around a weekly trip to the "big bathtub," the ocean, each weekend. Each couple is building its own cathedral around its own needs.

The rites of love embrace our whole lives. We should remind ourselves again that love and sex are not limited to or even epitomized in sexual intercourse. When Billy Graham said recently, "I don't think there is sex in heaven; if you really want it, you'd better get it here on earth," he expressed perfectly and unwittingly the moribund sexual mores of the Victorian age. To him and apparently to his numerous followers, sex is some kind of troublesome appendage on life, but not rightly part of it. The view expressed here is that sex and love are inseparable and are central to human development. "The kingdom of heaven is within you."

Best of all, the rites of love are in every meaningful sense "contracts." They say to each partner: this is what we mean to each other, this is what we are aiming at. To the public at large, it seems slightly humorous that a couple should walk up the aisle with a baby in their arms. The couple might answer, under questioning, that they really considered themselves married when they began living together (this is the cliché of lovers ancient and modern). The "common law" states, of course, recognize this rubric as a legal fact. Yet the walk up the aisle is humorous only because it strikes a chord in human sensibilities as the *ritual* which somehow seems to be lagging behind the real contract. We know that the "real" contract has already been made. What we don't realize is that the ritual *is* the contract in this case, because it is the *acknowledgment before the community*.

The possibilities for extending the values of ritual in everyday life are endless. Perhaps it is because we are so embarrassed by "unsavory" rituals—such as the command performance a company president expects at his formal Christmas party, or the bureaucratic antics of the United States Congress—that we rebel at the thought of introducing ritual, let alone tolerating it, in our daily living. We have been warned repeatedly about "habits" and "patterns of behavior"—about getting into ruts and losing our individuality—perhaps to the point where we draw back from reinforcing such patterns if we seem to be letting ourselves open to criticism. For example, our friends might tell us that our old family recipe for lasagna could be improved by adding a new ingredient ("Why not try something different for a change?"). Change and growth only occur against a background of tradition and custom, even in such a trivial area as cooking! The big change that occurs in ritual-making is at the time of marriage. Husband and wife must each give up the patterns of behavior of their parents and friends, and form their own patterns, their own rites. "Mother, I'd rather do it myself" is the plaintive cry of the newly married woman that speaks of this basic human need.

The greatest release from Puritanism is not the release from sexual constraints, but liberation from the *enemies of emotion.* All of us can not only laugh and cry and dream and hope, but we can also make laughing and crying and dreaming and hoping unashamed parts of our lives. We can create a framework within which our emotions have a special meaning for us. We may not be right in thinking they are special, but their value as ritual is the same regardless of an objective measure. The measure of emotion is *us.*

The moral is this: make the most of all ceremonies, celebrations, and observances that come your way. See them as things in themselves. See them for their value to you—in allowing you and your loved ones to lead a fully *social* life. Create your own personal way of celebrating love and living. The cynics would eliminate everything from man's life except the rational; this is their *own* form of intellectual ritual. The Christmas tree is only a symbol, but it has stopped wars between nations and between lovers.

7 Value Added By Love

If romantic love is the legacy of the Age of Chivalry, a very strong codicil to that bequest is that love has a natural enemy in the institution of marriage. This is the current wisdom of youth. The "romance" countries of Europe have for centuries dramatized extramarital love as the only genuine article. American middle and upper class are comfortable in the opinion that it is sufficient to *like* your partner to sustain a relationship; indeed, most would say that love is an inebriation which one gets over in the sobriety of growing up.

Broad philosophical claims are founded on the supposed love-marriage polarity. In *Love in the Western World,* Denis de Rougemont leaves no doubt about the subject: "If our civilization is to endure, it will have to carry through a great revolution. It will have to recognize that marriage, upon which its social structure stands, is more serious than the love which it cultivates, and that marriage cannot be founded on a fine ardour." The revolution, sir, has already occurred.

The message of the social commentators is simple enough: marriage may aid and abet the love of two people but not the other way around. The logical extension of this point of view is that if we can only eliminate more of the "fine ardour" from the nuptials, we can establish a more lasting relationship. All discussions of the plight of American marriages begin with a recitation of divorce rates and usually end with a prescription for more practicality and rationality in the choosing of a mate. All of this is fine, except that I feel, in promoting practicality, the value of love—I would say even the *rational* value of love—is not given its leavening chance to help the marriage grow. Love may not be enough; but without it nothing else has a prayer.

In *Uncoupling: The Art of Coming Apart*, Marya Mannes and Norman Sheresky argue: "According to the latest report on marriage issued by the National Center for Health Statistics in the Department of Health, Education and Welfare, 455 out of every 1,000 marriages made in this country last year are destined to wind up in the bitter and unhappy toils of the divorce court. With our divorce rate now the highest in the world, obviously the time has come to ask what is wrong with the American way of marrying...." What is wrong, they conclude, is that it is too easy to qualify for the license; young couples are not required to think out their motivations in advance and to face the unromantic practicalities of "coupling." The thrice-married Ms. Mannes, who should know, wishes fewer people would undertake marriage to begin with.

I think it is hasty to conclude that the ease of getting into marriage is the chief cause of our "highest divorce rate in the world." Vis-a-vis Italy or France or Spain, the ease of getting *out* of marriage is superficially a far greater factor in our high divorce rate. Indeed, the rapid turnover in American marriages should have, by any logic, produced the greatest educational system possible for divorced spouses seeking to remarry. It hasn't. On the contrary, what I suggest is that closing the loopholes both into and out of marriage will not insure anything but more unhappiness and frustration—*without love*. Beyond this, I would suggest that love in itself is the most subtle of all contracts, and can be talked about in a rational way—yes, cultivated and made to grow in a conscious, cold and calculated effort.

The biggest single factor which I believe has been overlooked in the evaluation of the potential for love in marriage is the revolution that has occurred in the last two or three generations in the *availability* of that precious commodity. In the ancient and medieval worlds, especially in the period of the Industrial Revolution, it was just very difficult to find "loving situations." Survival was the first and usually the continuing requirement in everyday life. Now, love has always been the touchstone of poets and playwrights. But for the great masses of people time and energy were largely devoted to other pursuits. Romantic love was an idealized daydream.

So many other changes have occurred in our generation that the "love revolution" has been overlooked by social observers. The change that has taken place in our ability as a culture to "love one another" is far simpler than William Reich's Consciousness III. If anything, it is the antithesis of "future shock"; it is the result of greater leisure, more avenues of communication, and the freedom from debilitating competition. The lot of humanity has been enriched far more by this aspect of technology than by intercontinental or interplanetary travel. The moon is worth more as something to look at than it is to walk on.

Love has many aspects, from the love of a divine Being to the love of a puppy dog. Yet I think we could agree that the greater *opportunity* to love in our era manifests itself in just about all its manifold aspects. I maintain that people nowadays are more generous in helping the destitute. Foreign aid, admittedly not all inspired by love, would have been unthinkable in the Napoleonic or Roman eras. Social or political causes were supported by fear, not generosity. It almost seems ludicrous nowadays that a saint could have made his reputation by cutting his cloak in half. A Peace Corps would have been laughable only fifty years ago.

We resist the insinuation that human nature is really any different now than it was in the days of classical Greece. Our wars are no less brutal, or are they? Are we perhaps in that twilight between two vastly different ages, so close to both that we think people will go on justifying the force of arms or the killing of criminals on humanitarian grounds? Against this background I would argue that at the very least we know that man now has the potential for greater choices in his personal life. He is more mobile in the livelihood he prefers and the company he keeps. And the simple fact is that couples now choose to marry for *love* rather than for convenience or for financial security.

This is a fact that won't go away in any analysis of *why* people marry. Our whole culture proclaims it.

Now then, is this "love" I am referring to more than an emotional concoction of possessiveness, immature daydreaming, and sexual fantasy? Or is it that pure variety carefully delineated by the philosophers as "wishing well for the beloved?" The best measure of a culture that we have is the media that reflects it. I think the broad evidence is that at no other time in history have people been more open to each other—to new views, to controversial subjects, to psychological and social concerns. Today we are confronted as never before by all the pulls and pushes of emotion and personal gratification. Most commentators point to the dominance of sex in our visible culture; but all the other drives and aspirations of the human personality are also blatantly appealed to, for "good" purposes as well as for antisocial purposes. I feel a certain relief in the openness and good humor of the "man in the street," who willingly answers the most personal questions under his name and photograph in the daily newspaper. When asked if he prefers jogging to sex, the man in the street retorts that he prefers to jog to bed.

The healthiness of modern attitudes to personal, emotional concerns is the best assurance, in my opinion, of sexual equality. Everyone is caught up in assuring the equality of *tasks*. Claude Servan-Schreiber, in a recent article in *Paris Match,* goes to great lengths questioning a young couple who teach at Stanford University about their "marriage of equals." Yet the equality seems to consist largely in each having a career (earning money) and each doing household duties (playing house). A more basic equality is that which springs from "wishing well for the beloved." My point is that a healthy honesty about oneself, which is reflected in even the flip comments of the man in the street, is the *signal* of the ability to love.

All of the truisms about love bear repeating because they indicate how love can be *learned.* And if love can be learned, then it can add the finishing touch to the marriage contract. It is something that can be *done:* it is not a mystical gift or a happy accident.

The truisms are these: To love is to wish more for the other person than for oneself. (In sexual love, the desire to please your partner is so basic that all techniques and preparations are meaningless without it. This fact is the strongest argument against masturbation, with or without a partner.) To love is to *give* rather than to receive—another way of saying the same thing. To love is not to want to possess, or to be possessed. To love is to see the good in a person in spite of all past failings. It is no utopian dream that man can love his enemies; he mirrors whatever good he has in himself in a corresponding good in his "enemies." Conversely, the loudest and most self-righteous complaints a man has about another usually tell more about the faults of the speaker than of the object of his antipathy. These and other truisms can be enlarged upon indefinitely, and, although I am no lover of *The Prophet,* I think there is an abundance of worldly wisdom here and in similar books for anyone interested in trying to find out what love is all about. Why should there be an intellectual taboo about the study of love?

The first observation one should stumble upon in an examination of love is that it can be *created* just by "wishing it were so." To *try* to love is to love. If this seems like a mystic's view, conduct a little experiment on the purely social level of greeting acquaintances in the street. A smile and a good word are *observably* effective in bringing about exactly the same result from the other side. The same psychological phenomenon is the basis of Coach Woody Hayes' remark, "Show me a good loser and I'll show you a loser." The telephone company has documented that "smiling" voices are actually more helpful than "businesslike" voices. Human love is not so mysteriously different from a friendly smile. In its most complex, emotionally laden forms, love remains not a gift from the gods but a product of man's own making.

A second, more curious phenomenon about love is that it pleases the *giver* in direct proportion to how much love is *given.* The mournful wail of an unrequited lover is probably self-love at its most intense. "How can it be so good if it feels so bad" is the cry of one who is "in love" perhaps, but who really is a possessor rather than a giver. It is perhaps a cruel thought to suggest, but I believe that "crying one's heart out" is a good sign of crying for one's own lack of love. The other side of the coin is that the giver of love is somehow the beneficiary of his own gift. Perhaps the proper place to discuss such subjects is in newspaper columns. I leave it to the reader, however, to examine the evidence of his own life for a corroboration of this simple psychological fact.

Often two people perpetuate each other's need to be loved without realizing that they are stoking the wrong furnace. It takes real honesty to see when you and your lover are only playing at the love game, feeding each other's possessiveness. Two people can create a fantastic fiction, with all the trappings of gifts and dates and liaisons, only to discover that a genuine concern for the other was never really there. Or they can try to impress each other with "good deeds," with their social concerns, with their altruism. In the old film "Daisy Kenyon," the corporation lawyer dallying with Miss Stanwyk's affections volunteers to defend a penniless farmer as a gesture of his "goodness." He readily acknowledges his motives, but that doesn't change the motives. Significantly, Daisy misses all the cues of this false lover and only at the last moment sees the light. In real life it is all too parallel.

It is remarkable in our scientific age that just about every psychologist grants that "love at first sight" actually occurs. More than physical attraction, epitomized by the famous "glance across a crowded room," this sort of mystic experience defies conventional explanations. Is it possible that the shape of a man's back, the certain way a woman walks, or a few lines across one's face can tell, in an instantaneous glimpse, everything about a person, and cause one to give that person his or her lifelong love? There exists the ability of human perception to take in a complete scene in one gestalt, only one part of which is a girl's head. I leave it to speculation. It seems to me equally remarkable that two people are often not physically attracted to each other at all and only grow slowly to know that they love each other.

A final point about the paradoxical nature of love is that we can be rational *about* love without *it* being rational at all. The temptation always arises to dismiss the nonrational as nonhuman. It is nonrational to dine out, to buy flowers, to write poems. But the emotions are *not* necessary evils that will vanish in the cold light of day: that is the time when they are generally most needed. We *can* analyze love and how to create love in ourselves (which is to say, in others). It is difficult, for example, to seriously ask a person to "love God." We love what is tangible, not what is abstract. In saying over and over again that we follow the first commandment, we run the risk of merely being in love with the security of organ music and colorful vestments. Spinoza's heresy before the elders of the synagogue was to suggest that God must be material, not spiritual; and that the Bible never suggested anything more than a material, universal Being. The dramatization of the person of Jesus can create a love, a longing to be with him, a desire to give oneself to his work. But the admixture of personal traits with the abstract idea of a Supreme Being seems to me to lead often to confusion and disappointment. A theology which brings out a personal object of love, perhaps the embodiment of God in all human beings, can make a better claim to honesty in asking us to love God. Love, like faith, is not the product of our intellect but of our whole person.

A major suggestion of this book is that love can be protected by contracts and indeed *is* a contract in itself. I will be so optimistic as to suggest further that it is a self-enforcing contract, to continue the analogy. In a sense, there is no such thing as unrequited love. When your heart goes out to another person, when you give yourself to that person, a similar love returns to you. This psychological event is obvious on the "platonic" level of nurse to patient, grandfather to child, worker to fellow worker. It does not seem so clear in the case of a love that has the possibility of becoming sexual. What I am suggesting, however, is that the sexual element often introduces possessiveness and insecurity, and thereby confuses the issue. When love is freely given (according to the basic definition of "wishing well for the beloved"), it is always reciprocated, I maintain. And this, of course, is the perfect contract, the perfect quid pro quo.

Such a claim is not demonstrable and may even seem absurd in view of the typical deserted wife who avers, "I still love him." Can love be spurned? My guess is no. A possessive love, yes. But the real article recreates itself in ways that only novelists and poets have been able to describe. I would also suggest that the cynic observe the glow that transforms a woman's face when her engagement is announced, even though she has been living with her lover all the while.

The married couple who has lived quietly for many years, just getting by and perhaps struggling with a child or two, can discover the extra dimension of love quite by accident. They may have stopped playing bridge together or going to football games and parties; but the awareness of each other's needs dawns on them either in a moment of crisis or with the sudden realization that their growth as persons depends on each other. Love *is* the reaching out to each other at these moments. Or it can come as the love of a father for a son, long separated by a divorce and a remarriage of the woman. As Simone de Beauvoir has proclaimed, the age at which love comes is open, and can be accompanied by physical awareness to a degree never before really appreciated in our culture.

What happens when the contract based on love falls down? It is easy enough to say that "real" love never existed there before. Though I suggest that love has other apparently magical properties, I do not pretend that it is eternal. Growth and change are inevitable. There is no reason to believe that mutual love will always be enough to sustain a personal relationship, between man and woman or between friends. Of several divorces and remarriages I know of personally, all have seemed to work out better for all parties. In every case, love is most evident in the honesty with which each person is able to approach his or her new relationship. Other couples in my immediate acquaintance have been somewhat more patient in waiting for the right person the *first* time. In spite of Denis de Rougemont's pronouncement, they have waited for the "fine ardour" to appear, and they have been blessed by it.

We now come full circle. If love can be a value in marriage, can it be that much better *without* marriage? This is the crux of the question left by the Age of Chivalry, which has colored our attitudes for six centuries toward man, woman and love. I have tried to answer it by saying, first, that we are in a new age in which love is no longer the unattainable Holy Grail; it is plentiful for all who would have it. Second, I have proposed that love is only an enemy to marriage, or vice versa, because of our inability to deal with love rationally and practically. Marriage *is* the enemy of a possessive love, a love that depends on Cupid's darts. Love is, at the same time, the jewel in the marriage ring and the signet that binds the ring together.

8 Freedom From Money

Money is the symbol of the best of things and of the worst of things. We can at once admire the ideal of living "on love and pale moonlight" and the reality of bringing home the bacon. We know that the human spirit can overcome all the adversities of financial misfortune; at the same time we see evidence daily of the subjugation of the human spirit to the whims of financial circumstance. So when we hear it said that the chief obstacle to a successful marriage is money, in fact the most frequently cited cause for divorce, it should be obvious that we are not talking just about who controls the checkbook or how much money one earns, but about that whole mix of things known as "the human condition."

It's the human condition to have to find a place to live, to secure some sort of livelihood, to adjust to the conditions of one's employment, of one's neighborhood, of one's friends and fellow workers. A sort of inherited class system exists, even in this most socially mobile of nations, whereby the line of least resistance is for a son to follow in his father's trade, for one's life style to be determined by his early education, and for one's wife or husband to be dictated by economic background. Compare, for example, the disadvantage that accrues to generation after generation of poor families, especially black, who have never *inherited* anything for a century. Even the modest middle-class legacy of a mortgage-free home, a few stocks, and assorted heirlooms gives the typical inheritors a "cushion," usually in their middle age, which allows them in turn to pass on to their children a little bit of security in a threatening world.

The other side of this coin, of course, is the fact that the "security" of money can become an even greater ogre than the lack of it. And by this I don't mean at all the occasional case of the man who becomes obsessed by his inheritance, who sees it as a sacred trust and not as a negotiable commodity. I mean, rather, the more common obsession with money as the only stronghold in a competitive society. The threat of unemployment, the desire to keep pace with the possessions of one's neighborhood or social class, and the uncertainties of old age all create an atmosphere in which the very purpose of life seems to be just to *survive*.

Against this background, it seems to me that the basic freedom is *not* to have enough money, but to have enough motivation in one's life *beyond* money, that is, beyond the necessity of survival. A moment's reflection will convince you that this is no small order. It is, in fact, the whole purpose of philosophies and religions to generate alternatives to the accumulation of material goods as the purpose of life. Yet we know all too well that this effort throughout history seems an exercise in futility—a mere footnote or frivolous appendage to mankind's struggle for material survival. Even the well educated and the "inheritors" of the earth seem in general to be able to ignore the nobler sentiments of "other worldly" philosophies without peril at all to their equanimity. Yet I wonder.

In our own time, marriage is a good indicator of the ability of people to succeed or fail *as people*. Divorce attorneys commonly remark on the failure of two individuals *to grow up* as the persistent theme of early divorces. In other eras, marriage was not such a good measuring stick, simply because marriage was either artificially entered into or artificially prolonged. The judgment of marriage statistics in our time is that a large percentage of people have either failed as adults or are unhappy people. In other words, the attainment of security or the reliance on money as a motivation for living does not seem to have been eminently successful in our own very materialistic age.

Various figures are quoted on the failure rate of marriage. Two divorces are currently being recorded in California, for example, for every three marriage licenses. This statistic, however, loses some of its punch when you consider that there are several times more married couples than there are couples of marriageable age. We should also acknowledge that a marriage that breaks up after 20 or 25 years can hardly be considered a "failure"—except at the point when it breaks up, and at that point all kinds of mitigating circumstances are possible. The most meaningful statistic is that used by the Bureau of the Census: the number of divorces in an average annual period is equal to 40% of the number of marriages in a similar period *seven years earlier.* The seven-year time lag is the most likely duration of a marriage according to current figures.

When "money" is cited as the reason for divorce or separation (as it increasingly is—the first or second reason in about half of the 700,000 divorces last year), it is seldom "lack of money," but disagreement over its priority in the marriage. In the marriage contract, it is commonly known that "money management" is supposed to be the duty and prerogative of the man. In 20 states, mostly Southern but including Massachusetts, Pennsylvania, Vermont, Utah, and Alaska, property of any kind can be owned "by entireties." This means that husband and wife are considered such an entity that either one "owns" the entire property by himself or herself. This has the effect of requiring both signatures on documents, but also protects one partner from lawsuits on the other. Because a wife, for example, owns "the entire" property of her husband in these states, a creditor cannot make a claim against only the husband. In six other states, including New York and New Jersey, this applies only to real estate. But real estate is typically the most important tangible property a couple will ever own. The eight "community property" states, generally in the West but including Texas and Louisiana, vary in the practical application of the law regarding who owns what. But in California, for example, community property is strong enough as a legal notion to

Freedom from Money

prevent the bankruptcy of one partner to affect the other. Because of the great variations from state to state regarding legal title to property, it is often advisable to draw up contracts excepting certain property from common ownership, say, in California, so as to protect the assets of a well-to-do wife or to avoid complications in passing assets along to children. However, this type of contract rarely loses or saves a marriage—except in the sense that it assuages fears of an economic takeover by one of the partners.

Freedom from money, in the broader sense I am using here, is achieved by many couples in that self-examination of *motivation* which occurs in good marriage preparation. The foremost example of such preparation in recent times has been the "Cana Conferences" sponsored by the Catholic Church. Often ridiculed by youth and the old alike for the doctrinaire, dogmatic level of their programs, the Conferences nevertheless hold out an alternative point of view on the subject of *motivation.* Everyone who takes up the subject of marriage sooner or later comes to the conclusion that some sort of preparation must be made a requirement for obtaining a marriage license. After all, we require serious tests for a driver's license or for selling real estate. Worse yet, we assume a couple will make fit parents for any child they happen to procreate—but if they wish to adopt a child they must undergo careful scrutiny of their motivations and qualifications. In spite of all the talk about the necessity of marriage preparation, few attempt to do anything about it and the efforts of those who do are ridiculed.

Perhaps the couple should be forced to read at least one "marriage manual," a punishment which might be similar to Woody Allen's prescription of two days in solitary confinement with an insurance salesman.

In my opinion, the force of a contract shows itself quite important on this very point.

First of all, this is an area where a written contract can legally *extend* what is already implied in the marriage ceremony. Second, this is an area where couples can become very practical in a hurry. Money matters start out as very tangible, well-defined concepts, not clouded by idealism or romantic love. Finally, however, I believe discussion of money and material possessions quickly leads to their alternatives—to the area I call freedom from money.

The following is a suggested format for discussion of the money problem. It might even be considered an examination and might be administered as such. College students nowadays are quite familiar with seemingly endless entrance exams, scholarship tests, and aptitude questionnaires.

Preliminary Information

1. What does it take to "live comfortably" as a weekly salary (take home pay)?
2. What do most people make in my age and social group?
3. What does it take to operate a car annually? List four types of cost car owners have which non-car owners do not.
4. What kind of car do I find necessary for my way of life?
5. Is the status of an automobile important to us?
6. Would I be embarrassed arriving at a party or delivering my wife to work or children to school in a 10-year-old car?
7. Do I look forward to entertaining in a new home or apartment to show my friends I have "arrived"?
8. Other than that, am I proud to "do my best" for my wife or children by getting them the best living space I can?
9. Am I a better shopper than my wife? Does she look for bargains but waste money on convenience foods?
10. Can we afford to "eat out" every now and then, or should we save this money for our down payment on a home?

These questions are only indicative of a full list which could readily be prepared on the subject of money. These are written for a man to answer; a separate set should be devised for a woman. It should be obvious that the idea is to incorporate attitudinal questions in with factual ones. Although they are thinly disguised, the questions are designed not to trap the respondent but to make him rethink his values. If he lies to himself about his motivations, it only serves to bring him face to face with his inadequacy. On the other hand, if he can willingly say to himself that he wants money and all the trappings of success, he at least has had a chance to consider the alternatives.

The next step after the "examination," which should be drawn up individually, ideally by one partner for the other from a set of guidelines, the couple can then put down on paper what their motivations are and what they expect of their partners. These are some of the guidelines that have been successful in encounter groups and marriage preparation forums.

1. *Clearing the air*

    What property or other assets does either partner have which could cause some future disagreement or uncertainty?

2. *Management*

    Shall the couple work jointly on finances, or can one partner take the lead without offense to the other?

    Shall the couple keep all financial transactions on the table, or will either partner feel easier if he or she keeps his business or financial "deals" private?

3. *Goals*

    Can the couple change their goals as their circumstances dictate, without changing their basic marriage goal?

    Can the couple openly discuss goals—by means of discussing political causes, social issues, and so forth as they occur in the daily news?

4. *Work*

    Will the couple share the proceeds from work honestly, not downgrading the party who does not receive pay or who is paid less than the other?

    Can the couple consider changing roles or making a major change in the job of the "breadwinner" if he or she wishes a change?

5. *Recreation*

    Do the partners agree on the need for vacations or free time? Is there an open attitude toward the handling of money for their children's education and recreation?

If we think we can take most of such attitudinal changes for granted (after all, this is an enlightened generation in which the Peace Corps has more graduates than the Harvard Business School, and in which a Catholic missionary order recruits its men more successfully with ads in *Playboy* than in church journals), then consider what some of our "attitudinal" leaders think. The following invocation was reported by the New York Times as having actually been delivered by a Rev. J. Lawrence Yenches, D.D. of the Church of the Sea, Bal Harbour, Florida, to the banquet of the Florida League of Cities:

> Almighty God, we thank Thee for a free land where private property is a sacred reality. For millions it is not. Among us, Lord, are millions who own no home, no land, and no business. Owning nothing, they demand everything from a paternal government. Dear Lord, we fear they are potential victims for the panacea of Socialism.
>
> Help us, our Father, to remember that all we have—our schools, businesses, homes, banks, farms, mines, and building—are here because somebody worked for them and worked hard.
>
> Shake out the cobwebs among us, dear Lord, and give us a fresh look at ourselves. May there be enough problems to sharpen our wits and enough opposition to clarify issues.
>
> Bless all among us who work, produce, save, and invest, creating real wealth for our well-being.
>
> Help us to rely less on government and more on ourselves. Gird us to fight anything that destroys incentive, kills initiative, penalizes superior ability, and subsidizes laziness.
>
> Remind us strongly, O God, that without good business with a good profit, we can have no non-profit churches, schools, foundations, hospitals, tax-paid politicians, or a government giving away so-called free benefits or welfare subsidies.
>
> Preside at our meal: O Lord, sanctify our conversation, and may the glow of Thy Presence shine on all our faces. In the Master's Name. Amen.

If this is the motivational background of a couple, then let it at least be spelled out. I would suggest that if sufficient opportunities are not raised in the daily press to consider what one's attitudes to life really are, then the "life style" magazines should be read and talked about. It is more decisive of a point of view to read a copy of *Esquire* or *Harper's* than to read all the marriage preparation books on the market. It is equally helpful to engage in after-dinner conversation with one's elders—and to challenge them; or to challenge the sermon at your local church; or to challenge cocktail party truisms. We learn most when we are not "engaged" in learning. We learn more about ourselves from others than from introspection.

My wife and I once agreed that if I hired out to her as a handyman and if she hired out to me as a housekeeper, between us we would support our family quite well. This is the essence of bootstrap economics. But it's not that absurd. Why is the value of what we do measured by an "outside" standard? Why must an income be measured by how much a person contributes to corporate profit or to society? A family cannot be totally self-contained; even my father's and my grandfather's family, self-sufficient agriculturally, had to make a semi-annual trip to town to buy (or exchange) barrels of salt and flour and lard. Going outside the home to make a living is now taken for granted. What is not so clear is what this has done psychologically to the one who goes forth and the one who sticks it out at home, usually with kids.

The word "matrimony" has retreated slightly to the background because of the implication that marriage is merely a protection for the "matriarch"—a set of obligations designed to keep the vulnerable role of the mother safe from the callousness of men. Now, marriage is recognized as a partnership—especially in the field of money. What was merely contractual before has become influenced by the deeper, less legalistic contract of a social bond. And here again we come back to the point that contracts exist in forms we least expect; we can amplify their effects merely by becoming aware that they are *there.*

Here is a representative sample of contracts affecting the general subject of money which are *implicit* in what we do in the ordinary course of living:

(1) In more than 30 states, husband and wife must jointly sign many documents regarding property, life insurance, savings accounts. When the life insurance salesman tries to corner both husband and wife with the implication that the husband and wife must measure his love of his family in terms of what he

"provides" for them, it is time for the wife to say what she thinks of this. Does she play the passive role of "dutiful survivor," or does she consider the greatest disaster to be the loss of her husband (period), let whatever may come later, come? Does she put in her two cents worth on arrangements between her husband and his business partners? Or does she assume that "he knows best"—even though the short-term results of his "deals" are likely to be more important to her than life insurance or the purchase of a home? Does she concur in ventures in stocks and bonds—or does she let her signature be signed for her? Does she feel that her husband must bear alone all of the problems, reverses, and successes of his life—whether it amounts to a "big sale," getting a new job, becoming a union leader, or being personally demeaned by his boss or fellow workers?

On the other hand, does she feel that to share in her husband's financial success or failure is in itself an admission of subservience? Can she control her future only by being personally responsible for financial success or failure—in a job of her own or in decisions of her own?

The contract is there: it is a matter of doing something about it. The opportunity to do something usually occurs after marriage. But the search for motivation usually begins then anyway.

(2) A second contract which already exists, and need be only brought to the surface, is the *budget*. Theoretically, common law and later interpretations have held that the man is the manager of finances. How does it work out in practice? Some wives take the paycheck and dole out an allowance; others accept "house money" from the husband's take-home pay, and don't worry about what happens to the rest. The field is obviously open for an agreement. But few get down to brass tacks; most let habit take its course.

Knowing that the "legal" contract calls for the husband to be the provider, a couple can work out any number of valid, supporting contracts to amplify or alter this state of affairs. It can even be drawn up by a lawyer, but of course need not be. The truth is that no one takes money seriously enough until the breaking point comes.

Husbands who have had "amicable" divorces over other

matters—the raising of children, sex, etc.—are apt to hold to a close "survival" relationship with their ex-wives on the subject of money. The wife eschews alimony; the husband continues to help out when the house needs repairs or when she moves. The strength of the financial involvement of wife and husband cannot be overrated. This natural bond can be deepened by discussion and forethought.

(3) A third area where husband and wife already have contractual obligations over "money" is the care and raising of children. Too late many parents come to a breakup over the handling of adolescent children. It almost seems as if the growth of children in one direction or another crystallizes the attitudes of the parents—rather than vice-versa. Teenagers adopt the lifestyle of a sub-culture. The husband approves (even if along the grounds of least resistance). The wife sees this change of direction as a threat to her whole personality. But it may not be even a change: the seeds were always there. Young children may suddenly become to a woman the very expression of "living in the suburbs." She may rebel at the thought of raising them herself.

The obligations to children may be bonds which are tighter than money. But children represent only one aspect of "motivation," out of a totality of reasons for existing. To perpetuate one's lineage, to exhibit fecundity or "machismo," to belong to a social structure which encourages large families, such as the American-Irish, all of these are reasons for having children as way of life. This life is what it means to survive, as much as the accumulation of stocks is the meaning of survival for others. "Gather ye not into barns" is the admonition which applies equally well to both. "Store up for yourselves, rather, treasures in heaven."

(4) Finally, we all sign contracts, married and unmarried alike, by which we commit our futures to certain possessions. To own a home, to find a vacation property, to underwrite a business, to enter a profession—all require foresight and commitment. We express our values in living by our dedication to these commitments. We have all made our accommodation with the Biblical prescription "Sell all thou hast and give it to the poor." Like St. Martin, it is easy for us at a given time to cut

our cloak in two for the poor, but we "realize" that we also have our obligation to *ourselves*. Regardless of our extraworldly values, therefore, we plan for our earthly success. In this planning, we contract with each other to carry out these goals. The contracts may be in the form of deeds of trust, or student loans, or understandings of the hardships which must be borne to achieve success in our undertaking.

Others make contracts to live another kind of life: not necessarily dedicated to a profession or to a material goal, but to an ideal. The ideal may be as simple as the understanding that a wife shall pursue her talent as an artist. Yet all along the line, this understanding is reinforced by financial agreements. Even if he is not well educated in painting, for example, a husband will agree to work for his wife's success in that field. The point is that the terms of a contract are there—the quid pro quo. There is no neccessity for formal ratification of the contract. But if both parties think of it as a basic agreement, they can enhance it. In practical terms, they can talk with others about their goals and they can make their home a living demonstration of their understanding. No one will doubt their intentions.

Most couples wrestle with the problems of survival most of their lives. They are consoled by humorists who say, in effect, we're all in the same boat. A good many couples achieve a freedom from money (from possessions, from self-interest) which always amazes the cynic. Yet the cynic does not realize that money (and possessions and self-interest) are *not* the *opposites* of idealism. They are on two levels. Two people can be free of the burden of having to worry about survival even if they are in great danger of *not* surviving. The message of this chapter is that what it takes for this kind of freedom is the *recognition* of obstacles and opportunities, and not their blind acceptance.

On its most trite level, O. Henry worked this theme to perfection in his short stories. Husband and wife accepted each other with all their financial flaws because they were able to ignore the flaws. It is easy to retreat, from time to time, from reality in our own lives, but we cannot make it stick. We all worry about money, and possessions, and what others think. We can accept the loss of a friend easier than the theft of a valued piece of furniture. Yet we can look beyond this merely *by sensing this attachment as a contract.*

Shall we contract with things or with life? We answer the question daily.

9 Write Your Own Ticket

We have now seen a variety of ways in which "marriage contracts" are written without the two parties even being aware of it. What all of this suggests is that we have an embarrassment of riches. We started with the idea that the agreement we make when we say "I do" is inadequate, and we end by finding that all along we make very workable contracts through letters, dialogue, sex, ritual, expressions of love, and financial decisions. What more is needed?

The same question might have been asked at Appomattox, at Versailles, or on the U.S.S. Missouri. What is needed is a formal treaty. The comparison might well be taken one step further: what is needed is a *peace* treaty. In this case, the treaty signifies, not the end of hostilities, but the end of doubt and the beginning of the peace that comes with mutual understanding. That it should be in writing is part ritual and part psychology. It is also, like a shopping list, the best way to remember what you're supposed to be doing.

On the following pages are two sets of advice: first, on how to write a contract that will stand up legally yet not be sheer legalisms; and second, on what subjects to cover.

I implore you again not to treat a marriage contract as if it were a feminist manifesto. It is an old axiom that an unfair contract diminishes *both* parties. A racist economic and social pact shrinks the freedom of both white and black; a sexist inequality restricts both men and women from realizing their potential as people. The man who, because of our social compacts, cannot spend time with his children or enjoy his home is as impoverished a human being as the woman who is forced to believe she can do nothing else but be a "homemaker." Historically, right up to this day, marriage contracts have been proposed as ways of freeing women from the role of homemaker. In the otherwise admirable proposals of Susan Edmiston, Marya Mannes, and Alix Shulman, one gets the impression that all would be well if we could only solve the problem of housework. Even the working woman takes on the role of homemaker in the office—fetching coffee, watering flowers, doing errands—and this too "must be changed." The truth at the bottom of these complaints, however, should not be obscured by writing a contract which says, in effect, "share our misery."

Clare Boothe Luce, in a remarkable interview recently on the subject of women's lib, expressed the sentiment that women want to be homemakers, by and large; they don't want to compete in a man's world. Yet it is as difficult to accept the opinion of a dramatist, author, actress, and Senator on this subject as it is to sympathize with Eunice Shriver's feelings about abortion.

The point is that a contract which turns on a feminist-anti-feminist fulcrum is a marriage contract *second* and a manifesto *first*. Like all manifestoes, it is more a call for general reform than an instrument for personal use.

The following general rules are intended to help you write a personal document that would have legal force:

First, the agreements are to be extensions of, rather than retractions from, the existing provisions of marriage laws. For example, common law requires husband and wife to provide mutual emotional and physical support. A contract can spell out how they intend to carry this out in the division of labor.

Second, the terms of any agreement should not be so specific that compliance would be virtually impossible. If a husband agrees to wash the kitchen floor every Saturday morning (as part of the division of labor), the chances are the agreement would be violated every third week in football season; or perhaps the couple would take up golf, or sailing, or skiing and would not wish to take up part of the weekend in household work. It is not enough to say that the *intention* was good. Unrealistic terms could make a contract frivolous (and we are not talking here about the psychological value of a contract, but legal force).

Third, the contract must not attempt to overturn or evade existing interpretations of marriage law. Various writers have noted that a marriage agreement is not a simple handshake between a man and a woman, but a *ménage à trois* in which the state seems to throw considerable weight around. As we have seen, "public policy" dictates that a couple be monogomous, domicile together, and be responsible for their children, if any. So a contract which places a time limit on even a childless marriage is currently invalid. Worse than being invalid, it is entangling and divisive. Either party, in a "no fault" state, might find this sort of contract evidence of irreconcilable differences.

Fourth, the agreement should spell out what would happen when and if the contract were broken. Serious parties to this type of agreement would hardly "throw out the baby with the bathwater" over a minor breach. A contract which is strictly drawn is usually strictly interpreted by the courts. Therefore, the wording should be loose enough so that the dissolution of a marriage would result only from repeated or intentional neglect of the major contract terms.

Finally, the form and wording of the contract should *not* be patterned after the usual legal document. Good form is what is acceptable to a judge; good wording is what is clear. In all the marriage contracts I have seen so far, there is a conscious, almost pugnacious, attempt to emulate other legal documents. A contract for the sale of an automobile is less restrictive and verbose by comparison. In a field as new and open as this, there is every reason to avoid the rigidity of familiar sales contracts and business agreements. In particular, the wording can be positive and enlarging rather than restrictive, emphasizing what the parties wish to accomplish rather than where they might fail. Above all, the language must be the language of the parties, not of lawyers.

The following marriage contract is proposed as an example of both form and substance. The subjects covered go beyond what two people might normally require; they are shown here merely to indicate the range of possibilities to consider. The substance of the agreement is the existing marriage contract, as read by the "witness" or justice of the peace, and the usual interpretations of courts. The reason for this is simple: it is much easier to remedy an inadequate contract, certainly to enlarge upon it, by starting from it rather than by starting from scratch. The form, of course, is nothing like the traditional ceremony nor like a legal document. We will call it:

A Letter of Agreement

We, John Adams and Mary Brown, take it upon ourselves to put in writing the reasons why we wish to be married and the terms under which we believe it will be a successful marriage.

We do this as a result of our desire to remain married to each other under all circumstances we can reasonably expect.

We put our thoughts down in writing because we think we will respect our duties more carefully if they are more carefully spelled out. We fully realize that this letter has legal effect in so far as the violation of the spirit of this agreement would be evidence of irreconcilable differences or would be normal grounds for divorce or dissolution of marriage in the state we may happen to live in.

We feel that the periodic review and updating of this agreement is the best way of keeping on our course.

With these preliminary thoughts in mind, we wish to state our understanding in the crucial aspects of our marriage as they appear to us at this time. These aspects are (at present, to be enlarged upon in the future): our involvement with each other's interests and problems; our personal ambitions and ideas of achievement; our attitudes toward society at large and toward immediate friends and relatives. We think that these aspects of our relationship determine whether or not we "like each other," and if we like each other we feel we have a basis for respect and love. Under these three general topics we feel we can mention several specifics:

(1) Our respect of each other's time and personal needs, such as the need for self-expression, for recreation, for relief from the pressures of work at home or in an office, for dignity and pride.

(2) Our sexual honesty and commitment, in that each of us is willing to open himself and herself fully to the other, without fear of any use of such intimate knowledge to the disadvantage of the other.

(3) Our willingness to leave parents and relatives geographically and emotionally behind, in order to devote ourselves totally to each other.

(4) Our understanding that we will both work within existing economic and social conditions to maximize our joint potentialities and income, in short that we will recognize the inequalities of the current system of employment as an expedient rather than a measure of each other's basic worth. We will take every opportunity to advance the income and career potential of each other.

(5) Our willingness to sign a financial agreement (as detailed separately) if there are sufficient reasons to keep those assets isolated from our personal relationship.

(6) Our desire to have children, but to limit them to the capacity of each of us to care for them properly and to make them a part of our lives. This provision includes our understanding that the husband cannot absolve himself of the responsibility for the choice of family size.

(7) Our freedom to move to the place best suited to our mutual happiness, taking into account employment, climate, opportunities for both, and family development.

(8) Our willingness to adjust to changing circumstances in the management of day-to-day finances, so that neither party will be reduced to a fixed allowance nor be made to feel guilty or inadequate if there are financial setbacks, costly mistakes, periods of unemployment, unexpected illnesses, or other deprivations—in short we are serious in taking each other for richer or for poorer, in sickness and in health.

(9) Our understanding of each other's religious beliefs and

ideas about the values of life, including social concerns, public morality, economic justice and personal ethics; we have discussed each other's ideals and opinions and recognize areas of disagreement as well as of agreement.

(10) Our need for personal privacy and for personal accomplishment that cannot be totally lost in our attempts at mutual understanding and honesty with each other.

There are also specific circumstances in our past lives and future expectations which we feel it is important to record here, not to be limited by them but to look back on as a measure of our progress: (a) present ideas about the family, raising children, adoption, caring for parents, allowing relatives to help or advise us, education in the home; (b) existing friends and their importance and compatibility to both of us; (c) living habits and "life style" in food, clothes, manners, and acquaintances; (d) physical involvements that should be explained to each party, down to the embarrassing details, if necessary.

We therefore agree to live together with our obligations to society in mind; to renounce all others with our feeling for Christian or Jewish or Eastern religions in mind; and to honor and respect each other in the best traditions we revere, and to this purpose we sign our names.

_____

_____

This is the love contract. It can be helpful; it is not a panacea. It can help love flower and accordingly help love partners grow to their maturity.

Epilogue: Is Monogamy Obsolete?

A unique feature of the traditional marriage contract is its *open-ended* character: it is entered into on the presumption that it will be life-long. Such a presumption is obviously changing; the "trial marriage" of former years is no longer merely an experiment. The most society expects now is a "serial monogamy," one spouse at a time. Perhaps the real presumption has been, for a long time, "till death do us part, or until we decide to part."

Life-long monogamy is defended, when it is these days, for a variety of conflicting reasons. The Biblical prescription, "What God has joined together, let no man put asunder," is adhered to by the orthodox Christian churches, and by other religions in different words. The appeal here is to a "revealed" authority—to an other-worldly ethics. Others cite a political basis for their belief in monogamy. They would argue that the family is the nuclear unit of society, and the stability of larger institutions demands a stability in the family that only monogamy can guarantee. Still others point to the psychological relationship between personal maturity and the ability to sustain love. The persuasiveness of these arguments depends heavily on the marital experience and current marital condition of the reader.

What I would like to do here, rather than argue for or against monogamy, is instead make the case *for not abandoning it as a desirable goal.* This is a big difference. The easiest conclusion to reach—and it is reached and preached by psychologists, counselors, and judges as the current wisdom—is that monogamy, like a fine wine, is good to those who like it and not to those who don't like it. What I am saying is, in effect, that maybe more would like it if they were persuaded it is a desirable goal, that there is some sort of a pot at the end of the rainbow or at least along the way for them. In other words, perhaps a taste for monogamy can be developed if it were only sufficiently sampled.

Secondarily, I would like to make the point that "monogamy" covers a whole range of values other than "sticking it out" with one partner for one's entire life. Monogamy is not merely endurance: it is intensity and concentration. To be committed to a single person is to expect one's self-fulfillment in exploring the human nature of that person in depth, rather than in searching for a less intense but apparently more varied relationship with two or more people. The cynic's reply is that you can't eat the same meal every day, and that the way to buy a pair of shoes is to try some on until you find one that fits. Unfortunately the usual discussion of monogamy degenerates into such superficial analogies, which are about as meaningful as a fortune cookie. *Monogamy is more a state of mind than a spoken vow.* The better word for it on the biological level is the technical description "pair-bonding," but for reasons of simplicity I will stick with "monogamy" for the moment.

The religious, the political, and the psychological arguments for monogamy which I have mentioned above are typically of little help when a marriage reaches a breaking point. True, the pressures of relatives to preserve the appearances can be severe. The ego fantasy of not wanting to admit failure may also be a factor. But all of this is usually swept aside in the dynamics of two people facing each other and not liking what they see.

If the traditional arguments have little effect on the personal level, it is equally true that they just don't stand up on a demographic level. The simple fact is that people make mistakes, and usually greater ones when the stakes are greater. In general we admit that it is better to correct a mistake than to live with it. Personal experience seems to indicate that "second marriages" are reasonably successful, even though it is difficult to measure "success" on a statistical level.

The traditional arguments for the traditional marriage contract are so weak, in fact, that it is surprising monogamy has survived at all. It would be my guess that the chief motivation in many monogamously pure marriages is simple inertia. The cost of divorce in psychological readjustment as well as in dollars and cents pretty well keeps people in their ruts, no matter how unbearable it may seem at times. What kind of an ideal is inertia?

Having agreed to all of this, we have to recognize that there are values in traditional monogamy which are hardly self-evident in the early years of marriage. Some of the values are based on the biological nature of man, some on the nature of society as a whole, some on the psychological needs of individual people. In this Epilogue, I would like to make the case for these values in such a way that they add up to an ideal, that is, something worth striving for even if never fully achieved.

The alternatives to monogamy, of course, are more than the traditional patterns of divorce and remarriage, "common law" marriage, premarital sex, casual adultery, or simple "living together." Group marriages of from 3 to a dozen people, communes, and time-dated marriages are currently proposed by serious sociologists as the wave of the future. Scarcely a week goes by without one "authority" or another claiming that "by the year 2000" we will accept these forms of the family as readily as we now accept the "new morality." At present, however, the evidence is that the underground movement in the direction of group marriages is highly exaggerated, and has its counterparts throughout history under different guises in different societies.

Whatever the alternatives to monogamy, the case must be made for monogamy as a value in itself, rather than in comparison with its alternatives. For there will always be another "alternative" if the one under discussion doesn't appear to stand up well against monogamy. In other words, "proving a negative," namely, that the alternatives to monogamy are inferior, can never be fully convincing.

What follows is hardly a "proof," but a sequence of discussion leading up to the proposition that the monogamous state is both natural and beneficial to human beings. This proposition, if true, is a most fundamental consideration in a marriage contract, and has the potential of truly *liberating* a personal union. For what I have tried to make clear throughout this book is that "liberation" only results from knowing who you are and what is good for you. As James Hitchcock has said, there is a remarkable tendency for what is permitted to become required. A "liberation" based on permissiveness opens the doors to a more terrible tyranny of fashion, indecision, and aimlessness.

Whether the reader is convinced or not by the following line of reasoning, it is difficult to see how a contract of any lasting significance could be written or conceived without examining one's attitude toward monogamy.

I
Monogamy Is Not An Ethical Issue

We are accustomed to thinking of monogamy in religious contexts, and so we naturally assume it is an ethical question. Indeed, one who subscribes to the religious authority of a church or moral system which prescribes monogamy has made it a moral issue for himself, by definition. Yet no major religious denomination contends that to be monogamous is somehow in the nature of things—or, to put it the other way, that to get a divorce is an evil in itself, a violation of nature.

Consider what it means to say that something is "evil in itself." Is the taking of life such an evil? Is lying always wrong? Evil, on the contrary, exists in intentions, not in things or in actions; it does not exist without responsibility. If polygamy in whatever form is not an evil in itself (what an understatement nowadays!), does it nevertheless have ethical ramifications? That is to say, does polygamy violate a law—whether "God's law," "natural law," or any of the cornerstones of our ethical systems? Without getting into extensive debate on such a basic question, it is at least safe to say that monogamy has not always been "God's law" in the Judaic-Christian tradition; and that most societies have treated polygamy in its various forms as options open to human beings under the proper circumstances.

Monogamy is therefore really a social issue, that is, a concern of how people shall live en masse rather than how they deal with each other as individuals. It is on this theory, as we have seen, that the state (or society at large) claims the right to regulate the marriage contract, even to the point of encouraging or discouraging children. It may be against the law to be polygamous in New York State, but in establishing such a law the state is acting to preserve its social organization rather than trying to regulate the individual morality of its members. At the same we have to recognize that there is no clean line between what is "ethical" and what is "social." As James Hitchcock notes, "Laws embody a good deal of accumulated social experience, and people often appeal to the letter of the law to justify moral intuitions that they are not sophisticated enough to defend philosophically."

Once monogamy is recognized as primarily a social rather than an ethical issue, many confusing side issues are eliminated. We can face the question without becoming embroiled in religious arguments, based on traditional beliefs, and without making monogamy just an addendum to the whole issue of sexual behavior—which is indeed an ethical matter. One typical "red herring" is the claim that polygamy is right or wrong because it is the pattern or it is not the pattern in various cultures. But a social issue need not have a "right" or "wrong" side; rather, it is a question of a successful relationship between various individuals under changing circumstances. Thus a social question can be "situational" by definition, while the debate rages on over situational *ethics.*

Psychological and biological factors of course are intertwined in any discussion of monogamy. Just as the issue is not an ethical one, however, neither is it wholly a biological or psychological one. In short, there is no easy answer, based on a divine prescription or a history of man's sub-cultures or a study of his anatomy, to a question so basic to the nature of what it means to be human and to live in a human society.

II
Do Modern Conditions Doom Monogamy?

Changes have occurred so rapidly in our social organization over the last fifty years alone that we might well expect the whole pattern of our lives to be affected. If the patterns of marriage are basically social phenomena, it would be natural for new forms of marriage to occur at a time like this. Consider, for example, the new attitudes and changing economic circumstances affecting marriage that have taken hold in a single generation.

—Given the fact that a wife is no longer *essential* to the economic survival of a husband, as she was before urban life supplied 'labor-saving devices' and adequate services in the way of food, laundry, and accommodations...

—Given that children are no longer a labor source but a financial and personal inconvenience...

—Given that sexual mores and in fact morals have changed to the point where the phrase, "Why buy a cow when milk's so cheap?" is quoted daily by bachelors...

—Given that Americans are beginning to accept the idea, common in Britain for many years, that the absence of a wedding ring may make a man a *better* employee, boss, or whatever, instead of being "proof" that something is wrong in his head...

—Given that abortion and the acceptance of "love children" have made illegitimacy a dead issue...

Granted all this, is monogamous marriage in fact already an anachronism, a dinosaur on the edge of extinction?

Many current books have their sole appeal in this thesis, and have achieved "best seller" status. Wife-swapping is no longer an exotic perversion, but the subject of popular movies shown on television and of countless articles in "family" magazines and newspapers. Everyone seems to be able to quote how the

Eskimos live happily without any sexual jealousy or possessiveness. Infidelity is not only expected from a successful man, it is almost demanded by his peer group. The American culture seems headed toward the French or Japanese traditions where the lack of a mistress is proof of either low sexual drive, and therefore lack of "manliness" and basic energy, or of the inability to support a mistress and, therefore, a low economic position in society.

We seem to be "acting out," in other words, a proof of the thesis stated by Denis de Rougemont, the French theologian, in his book, *Love in the Western World*. M. de Rougemont examines the idea implicit in Western thought that passion and stability are incompatible in a "good" marriage.

> "Either a resigned boredom or else passion—this is the dilemma our lives come up against as a result of the contemporary notion of happiness. In any case this notion threatens the ruin of marriage as a social institution that is defined by its stability."

Stability in marriage seems now more a matter of the preservation of social position, particularly among the educated middle class, than any promise, or realization, of a true monogamy. So the ability to realize our "passion" in modern society would appear to doom the institution of marriage; and all that marriage shored up in past generations was the negative side of thesis—we accepted boredom and so achieved domestic stability.

We are being told, in effect, that only fools and cowards are monogamous and, in so many words, that man is "naturally" polygamous, that this is his current state of evolution.

It is this central assumption that is being examined and challenged in the following argument.

III
Is Increasing Sexual Freedom Necessarily a Sign of Progress?

While it has often been stated that the majority of *"cultures"* are in fact polygamous, it is generally granted that most of the world's *population* lives in cultures that at least espouse monogmass of anthropological data indicates that the lack of taboos amy as the ideal. But, more importantly, the overwhelming on intercourse with persons outside the married mate, after marriage has taken place, is roughly correlated with the nearness of the particular culture to extinction—or what might be called the "last days of Rome" theory. The lack of restraints are not the *cause* of the downfall of a culture, but a concomitant. Thus the Eskimos survive in an extremely hostile environment by loosening the bonds of fidelity ... out of necessity. The Tierra del Fuegans, on their way to total extinction as a people as well as a culture, drop all taboos including even those of incest. Pitrim Sorokin has formalized this observation into a theory that free sexual behavior is a sign of a civilization in decline.

Freedom from sexual constraints, then, seems more the result of a cultural desperation than of any great progress on the part of the society. And it has been amply demonstrated that war, famine, or anything that increases tension and arouses a fear of non-survival also increases sexual activity and lowers sexual inhibitions. Soldiers in combat and executives under corporate fire share this phenomenon. The need to copulate is aroused by fear far more than by a sense of security. Perhaps we can fairly say that the fear of death indirectly encourages the desire to procreate. There is substantial evidence that the death of a central family figure, a patriarch or matriarch, tends to increase the birth rate of the surviving children of reproducing age who are strongly affected by the event.

It is not necessary to prove that sexually promiscuous societies are the cause of a political downfall. The point is simply that sexual "liberation" is no sure sign of cultural maturity.

IV
Marriage as the Ultimate "Life Style"

Marriage is a choice to *share,* in all senses of the word, your life with another life. No other single choice, even including the choice of a career, is more determining about how you will live for the rest of your life—about what kind of person *you* will become. This other person is not just a business partner or friend; he or she is going to affect how you feel about yourself in open and unconscious ways fully as much as your parents.

Ideally, then, we are "acquiring" a mate who will release us from loneliness, help us make our way through life and provide a source of strength that will help us function better in every part of our lives. A good mate is the most valuable "asset" that either husband or wife will ever have.

In simple terms of choice of "life style," most human beings prefer to have someone around than to be lonely. Loneliness seems as central a fact in our thinking about man as his sexuality or his aggressiveness.

We human beings seem to be very rarely more happy alone than when we have someone to share our sorrows, our triumphs, our stresses, and our life experiences in general. This sharing gains in value with longevity, and in fact seems to have little significance without the continuity of a long-term relationship. Are we begging the question already? Is it possible that the values of "life long sharing" can be secured in our modern world in other ways? Have we as evolving human beings learned to move faster from one relationship to another, assimilating old loyalties with new experiences without the old emotional involvements? Or are we pretty much from the same human cast as Homer's Odysseus, making the most arduous journey home from war in history to rejoin his loyal wife?

If human nature has not changed so radically over the ages, why have so many well-educated, sincere people nowadays abandoned the old ideals, and in fact proclaimed the "death" of marriage—the death of the life style of one to one associations and support?

Let us look at some of the forces which would make so many of our "opinion leaders" feel that marriage is out of date. Our point in this search is to see if the "life style" has changed, or if it is merely laboring against unusual pressures.

V

The Pressure of Rationalism

One of the great ideas of Western civilization is that of rationalism ... simply stated, that man can *think* his way to salvation, success, or even happiness. For example, psychoanalysis, according to a brilliant analysis in *Freud: The Mind of the Moralist*, was the result of Freud's saying, in effect, it is this damned *unconscious* (or irrational) that fouls us up. If we can just make the unconscious conscious, then we can really rule our lives in a "sensible, rational and reasonable" manner.

Rationalism taken to extremes is its own worst enemy: it is the serpent who began to swallow his own tail and is now reaching his own head. In seeking to demonstrate the existence of God "mathematically," it devoured the approaches to belief that formerly carried the greatest weight with the "full man." And a purely rationalistic analysis of man and his needs has been the godfather of political tyranny—whether from the socialistic side or the fascist side.

Everywhere we see the results. The growth of "psychopathic deviancy," the total lack of moral constraints, is one symptom. The notion appears concurrently with the "Don Juan Myth" in Western literature. The hero of Moliere's *Don Juan*, when asked in what he believes, replies, "I believe that two and two are four... and four and four are eight." This is the ultimate assumption behind the rather inhumanly logical form of our economy—a rule by statistics for the manipulation of people as numbers.

The burden of rationalism is its struggle to reduce two of the basic aspects of the nature of man—his animality and his spirituality—into the concept of man as a thinking machine. In trying to "pack" the rational suitcase with the parts of man that just won't fit there, rationalism has had to distort or leave out much of what man really is. He is an animal, and he is a free spirit.

VI
Some Kind of Animal

Before Darwin's sweeping guess about the development of man, there was no doubt in man's view that he was the center of the universe and "the apple of God's eye." Even now, the usual treatment of the theory of evolution is that man evolved *from* the lower animals—on *up*. It is rarely accepted that man *remains* an animal. The recent fad of "touchy-feely" therapies is an attempt to react against the still dominant notion that man is not really an animal but a fallen angel. Yet the idea persists that all man has to do, according to most of our rationalistic philosophy and theology, is to find the "right" set of thoughts and salvation will be waiting.

The new science of Ethology—the study of instinct—is beginning to offer evidence of how much an animal man is, and how important his animal nature is to his real "salvation." There is now reason to believe that his animal instincts, so far beneath what is usually called the "unconscious," still affect human behavior in a remarkable way. Desmond Morris, Jane Goodall, Robert Ardrey and Konrad Lorenz are only the most widely known authors of recent explorations into the instinctual roots of our behavior. These genetic influences, ancient and unfathomable by conscious self-examination, are instincts that we possess simply by being animal. The most widely studied instincts are territorialty and aggression. There are some highly interesting findings, however, which are now turning up about our mating patterns.

The concept of "pair-bonding" is one of them—the central notion that some species form an instinctively monogamous choice of a life-long mate, to whom each is forever faithful until death, just as in our old movies. They really do live "happily ever after" through all the trials and mischances of life, until death do them part.

While many authors, mainly anthropologists and psychologists in the great American tradition of environmentalism, may protest that man is a creature of culture, this prejudice—and that is what it is—is breaking down.

We are beginning to accept, very slowly, that we are truly, in every sense of the word, animals . . . and that this is not a condemnation or an insult, but a valuable way of knowing ourselves.

For example, the cerebral cortex, our "thinking brain," is the last major organ to evolve in man. Yet we have persisted in the belief that our bodies were designed for nothing but to

Epilogue: Is Monogamy Obsolete?

carry that little chunk of grey matter around, and that the brain should "rule" the body. This tool (which is what the brain is) is there to help us survive. We seem to have used it most effectively to help us kill our fellow men and make our lives unhappy.

In *Open Marriage,* Nena and George O'Neill, both anthropologists, proclaim this centrally important fact: the one-to-one relationship is a basic animal, and therefore human, pattern.

Man is the most adaptable mammal on the face of the earth. He has survived, even before science created artificial environments, from the Arctic regions to the Sahara. You must reach down into the parasites before you find such a diversity of survival situations ... and even there it only occurs because of the "artificial environments" provided by the body of a mammalian host.

It is obvious, also, that Man is the most adaptable animal culturally as well as physically. We can live in monogamy, polygamy, group marriage, "communal associations," serial monogamy ... almost any permutation imaginable ... live, survive and apparently prosper.

What is only now becoming clear is that there may be a "natural" mating pattern for man, and that it is probably monogamy. It is a truism in science that there are many possibilities open for animal survival. You can have a chimpanzee in a cage, in an "open environment" zoo, in a reserve, or in a natural state ... and his behavior patterns, particularly his courtship, mating, and aggression patterns, will vary enormously. But that form that produces the greatest apparent "well-being" is assumed to be the "natural" pattern.

Is there evidence, beyond our generalizations about the "naturalness" of pair-binding in animals, to indicate that monogamous marriage is the "happiest," therefore the most "natural," and therefore the most desirable of human states? Or does it not seem, as we are told in "Divorce, Italian Style," that the yoke of life-long marriage to one person has not really contributed to our general "well-being?"

VII
How Is It, Really?

In 1965, the sociologists Dr. John F. Cuber and Peggy B. Harroff produced an important analysis of American marriages "as they really are": *The Significant Americans: A Study of Sexual Behavior Among the Affluent.* Through interviews with over four hundred Americans, nearly equally divided between men and women, they evolved a set of "models" or ideas about the ways in which successful Americans reacted to each other in marriage.

They arrived at five basic kinds of relationships: The Conflict-Habituated; The Devitalized; The Passive-Congenial; The Vital; and The Total. Be patient with these ponderous titles; we will continue to use them in what follows as convenient labels, not to be interpreted from the names themselves.

Briefly, the Conflict-Habituated live in a constant state of quarreling and hostility although they frequently have great love for each other and are terribly upset if anything happens to the mate. The Devitalized had a deep love once and lost it to jobs, to other interests, and to the simple demands of daily living—to the point where they just exist together, either accepting the dullness or resenting it. The Passive-Congenial simply never let themselves become deeply involved in each other; they fear a loss of autonomy and so marry a partner who never threatens with attempted closeness. These are frequently the marriages that came about because of "similarity of interests," like careers, family connections, social status, and the triumph of the "reasonable." The Vital is characterized by the feeling that the important activities in their lives are important *because* they do them together. These are very deep friends and regard their time together as the most important and rewarding time they ever spend. The Vital is carried to its complete fulfillment in The Total. The Totally married share virtually every aspect of their lives.

The Total is the model of a truly "pair-bonded" marriage. Each helps each other in every way they can think of and, usually, feels that the other exaggerates how much they do. One

Epilogue: Is Monogamy Obsolete?

famous scientist, at considerable inconvenience, has been going home to lunch every day that he could for thirty years. He and his "friend, mistress and partner," as he describes his wife, have a quiet lunch and some conversation. They call them "our little seminars."

Dr. Will Menninger and his wife, Cay, maintained the half hour between 10:30 and 11:00 every evening for years to talk over the events of the day and family business. They called it "Menninger Time." Dr. Alfred Kroeber, the famous anthropologist, and his wife, Theodora, the now famous writer of Ishi and other books, had "family dinners" and "get-togethers" where everyone, regardless of how young, got his time to speak and was listened to with love, trust and understanding. A Berkeley psychoanalyst and his family, of my acquaintance, have shared their lives so completely that the children regard their parents as their "best friends"—a rare mixture or coalescence of personal and familial ties.

A typical partner in such a marriage, let's say a successful business man, reports, "I've wondered whether I was still attractive to women . . . even had a girl in bed once at a convention . . . I just looked at her, apologized and suggested I buy her a drink in the bar. For twenty years my wife and I have made love and we still keep discovering new aspects of each other and new excitements as lovers. Why should I take a chance on messing it up?" It reads like the plot of a dozen current films; but the question is, how do they do it and why can't everyone? And are Total marriages so rare as we think?

VIII
A Child Shall Lead Them . . .

Commitment to another person or to a set of ideals is the key to a Total marriage. What aids commitment? The example of how children are "committed" to their parents' love is a good starting point.

Our scientific rationalism culminated in the theory of psychology called behaviorism. This product of an American psychologist, John B. Watson, was an orgasm of the dogma of reason. Instinct and "heart" were rubbish; man came into the world a "tabula rasa," a blank slate, upon which environment would write to produce absolutely, with no other influences, the final result of what a human being became.

Watson came to be accepted as the new messiah, who would lead not only psychological theory but parents as well out of the dark ages of superstition into the Golden Age of rationality. Nearly ten years before the publication in 1928 of *The Psychological Care of the Infant and Child,* his theories reigned in almost every medical school in the country, and pediatricians who wanted to be "modern" swore by Watson.

This was the man who said breast feeding was wrong; mothers should not cuddle their children; never pick up a child just because he is crying, because it will spoil him; and, for heaven's sake, be the boss. Keep that kid on his feeding schedule. If you don't want a weakling later, enforce "logical" order and discipline right from the beginning.

The underlying assumption, of course, was that man was less an animal than a machine.

Dr. Harry Harlow is still working on a series of experiments with monkeys that began with the intent to find out if there was anything to the unscientific notion of "mother love." He raised several hundred infant monkeys with "surrogate mothers" formed of wire, sometimes bare and sometimes covered with terry cloth and supplied with a bottle "breast." The monkeys survived but the result was slightly horrifying.

The females would not breed. When forcibly impregnated, they would sometimes kill their infants. Sometimes they would instinctively feed the children and then hang by their tails from the top of the cage and bat at the infant as if it were an inanimate object. He concluded one interim report in "Nature" magazine by saying that he and his co-workers had speculated on the construction of a mechanical "rejecting mother," but they found they had inadvertently produced two hundred *real* ones.

Concurrently, particularly among some of our most respected intellectuals, there occurred an incredible misinterpretation of Freud's theories that came to be called "permissive upbringing." This travesty—really an aggressive trend—released

Epilogue: Is Monogamy Obsolete?

upon the world many very bright but tragically crippled children. Permissiveness was used as a "cover" for the mother's real statement, which went something like, "Go away and do whatever the hell you want to do. I don't want the responsibility of loving you, much less looking after you and helping you to learn self-control." Or, "I don't want to repeat what my father did to me." But the word has all but lost its meaning through misuse by friend and foe alike. To be permissive now is to be weak, unsure of your ideals. How far we have come! Poor Dr. Spock, who has just been trying to bring a little humanity back into the raising of these infant animals, is now saddled with the "permissive" label.

It was in 1946, with Dr. Spock, that we had a slight shift back to the human, the shift becoming more pronounced with each edition.

Now, all the new research indicates that Watson was exactly 180 degrees off the target. If you want a gifted, optimistic, happy, responsible and successful child, spoil him as much as you possibly can at first. Keep him next to your body as much as possible during infancy "just like an animal." Then when the time comes, he will not only accept responsibility but seek it as part of his normally maturing desire to expand his horizons, supported by the feeling of confidence built up by the security of his infancy. Feed him discipline slowly, but definitely give it to him. It is part of love.

One professor at a California college became interested in how one family had produced three sons and a daughter who were all happy, made top grades, were popular and athletic and seemed to be outstandingly healthy. He talked to the mother, an Italian immigrant woman, and asked her about how she had raised them. She said she didn't really know what she had done; she had just tried to be a good mother. But she gave as fine a capsule description as I have ever heard of how a mother should handle minor injuries like scraped knees, bruises, fights and the seemingly endless hurts of childhood. She said that she checked to see that it wasn't serious, washing away the dirt and tears and applying band-aids where needed, then she cuddled them for a little while, gave them something to eat and sent them back out into the world.

But think about all those children raised under Watson . . . they are now between 20 and 55 years old, depending on how old the mother's pediatrician was and how loyal to "science."

Do you still wonder why there are so many angry and emotionally frozen people in our generation and why so many people are afraid or unable to make a real commitment to another person? Or do you think it was always this way in preceding generations?

The human animal, like other animals, is only predictable in large numbers; in individual cases, there are always surprises. Harlow discovered one female monkey whose *instinctual motherhood* was so strong that she not only survived her traumatic infancy but took care of her own infant and of the infants of the "rejecting mothers" around her. You can mess up a lot with an environment, but you cannot, totally, destroy instinct.

IX
Learning to Give

Regardless of how we were raised, or how severe the old damage was, we still live in the here and now. It is stated here, as an article of faith with some slight support from the results of various forms of psychotherapy and transcendent experiences, that man can grow. As the most adaptable animal by any standard, man has always recovered from setbacks beyond anyone's expectations.

It is also stated as an article of faith that there are two main needs of human animals after they achieve survival security; the need to have a sense of autonomy and the need to feel that love and trust are possible. These are frequently made to be mutually exclusive, but they need not be.

The need for a feeling of autonomy can become a negative force in a human life when autonomy is seen as inconsistent with giving up of any of your own immediate wants and desires. This is called stinginess. When a human animal has not developed the conviction in childhood that love will be reciprocated, that person is afraid to give love for fear of not getting any love

Epilogue: Is Monogamy Obsolete?

back in return; or of actually being rejected, and therefore harmed, if committed love is offered. If a person is sure of his own "ownership of himself" he is not afraid to give of himself, but you can't give what you don't own.

The feeling that love and trust are possible comes, in its most natural evolution, from loving parents. In lieu of this good fortune, it must be learned in later life. And the only way to learn it seems to be to try it and find out. It is not always easy, and some realistic caution needs to be exercised, but it can be done.

X
A Return to Spirituality

Our time is involved in an almost frantic search for "belief," the ironic result of several centuries of the dominance of science. Rationalism has nearly destroyed, particularly for the highly educated, the spiritual value of the church. The church backed away from the direct experience of the "mystical" and trained priests to be thinkers, not feelers. The loss, unfortunately, has left a whole generation with only "the reality of the physical" to believe in. The ultimate manifestation of this trend is the Communist doctrine of dialectical materialism, the rule of man and society by strictly "logical" and "scientific" rules . . . as if man were a machine, in the guise of an animal.

This is the true "revolution" of our time and our youth. This is the cry voiced so clearly by James Dean in the movie "Rebel Without a Cause." When he rages at his father he is saying, Damnit, believe in me so that I will be able to believe in me, in you and in life itself.

Communism and socialism are not seductive to our youth because of their logic, but because they offer a dream to believe in . . . the dream of the classless society based on the hope that men can someday, somehow, rediscover a sense of community. And by "sense of community" they mean both a "love and trust" they still need from their deprived childhoods and a sense of a mystical belief to live by as adults. That they have so frequently chosen what is in itself a rationalistic idea—community—is only a testament to the continuing strength of rationalism and to the lack of other choices.

But other choices are becoming available. Everywhere we see the rise of mystical cults, systems, philosophies, and religions. From astrology to transcendental meditation to dope, we see our youth reaching out to see if they can't find *something* out there that is more than a materialistic, rationalistic shuck. They feel that they have been conned, and they blame it, frequently, on their parents. And, of course, those poor parents are not to be blamed—because they were the biggest suckers of all. Mistreated in childhood, driven to pursue the material, made to believe that the "American Way" was based on "success," the parents have been complaining about their lives for years. Now they are angry because their children listened to their complaints and are saying that they will not repeat the mistakes of their parents.

Thus the flood of "irrationality" in our time is not only the symptom of the disease, but, like a fever, an instinctive, natural attempt at healing. The cults, the retreats, even the orgies, are an attempt to break through the barrier of alienation that has cut us off from ourselves, from love and from life itself.

That these various communal activities frequently involve ritual is only natural. Confucius was once asked what the Rites for the Dead did for the dead. He replied that we could not know about the dead—we should concern ourselves with what the Rites for the Dead did for the living. He neatly summarized what sociologists are now rediscovering; that there are divisive forces and cohesive forces always present in every society, and that ritual brings men together in a cohesive way and makes them feel closer to each other and less lonely.

That these same "rites" are important in a successful marriage is obvious. "Menninger Time," "our little seminars," and the Kroeber's family meetings are ritual . . . frequently even to having set times. That saying Grace made God favor the family is, perhaps, questionable; that it made the family feel more together as a whole is obvious.

We have removed the rites and rituals from marriage. It is up to the new generation to restore them and teach us.

The rejection of the mystical and the animal by rationalism

is also partly to blame for Victorian morality. By denying the animality of man and rejecting the mystical qualities in sex, we began to speak of it as an "animal act," and therefore bad.

Thus rationalism, by denying both the animal and the spiritual, denied us also the benefits, the real benefits, of monogamous marriage.

And the return to spirituality, oddly enough, is made possible by a return to our animality. These odd bedfellows are the hope of the return to successful marriage.

XI
The Support of Monogamy

Dr. Cuber's study of marriage types in America is remarkable in that the book does not contain any statistics or percentages. However, a magazine article, done shortly after the publication of the book, revealed that the Vital and Total Marriages discovered in the study made up roughly one quarter of all the marriages. Even more surprisingly, nearly ten percent of these highly successful people had Total marriages. That this is far above the percentage of such marriages in the "normal" population is self evident. Remember, it was a study of "the affluent."

The conclusion is that successful marriages help in making people successful in everything they do. This is not really surprising. While we might assume that success follows success, it is also true that a successful marriage releases a store of energy for use out there in the "real world."

The Total marriage makes up a "Support Group" that increases the effectiveness of both people. Frequently the ideal of marriage is symbolized by two people, usually the pioneer and his sun-bonneted wife, standing side by side as two independent people working together. It is like the old proverb, "Love is not gazing into one another's eyes, but standing shoulder to shoulder looking at the same goal in the distance." Some Total marriages are like that. But it is not the only model for a Total marriage.

None of us is perfect and some of us are quite a bit farther from the ideal than others. The old French saying goes, "In every love, there is one who loves and one who allows himself to be loved," a classically cynical statement from the nation that was the midwife of rationalism.

An alternative is what I call "the True Triangle." This is the marriage where each leans on the other, sometimes one taking most of the strain and sometimes the other picking up the burden. Rooted on the earthly base of their physical existence, they each form one upright of the triangle . . . the strongest of construction forms. Of course it is only a weak analogy for a very complex psychological relationship. But perhaps the dynamics of engineering and psychology are not so different. Stress, in the engineering sense, creates strength in every dimension of an object.

Why not three people forming a tripod? Too often, almost inevitably I believe, the time will come when two legs will put all the weight on one and the tripod will collapse. It is a simple question of "Ego economics," and one example of the danger of gratuitous analogies!

The most important element in making marriage "work," after basic trust and respect have been established and acknowledged and the "support" structure agreed to, is the clear recognition that sacrifices will be necessary. We are perfectly willing to accept that sacrifice is necessary in occupations, in athletics, and in our daily life out in the "real world." This is taught us in school.

But too few people seem prepared by their parents or the world at large to recognize that sacrifice is all important in marriage. You give up many desires and minor ambitions in order to be able to get the reward of the support and togetherness that marriage can provide with a truly compatible mate.

Cuber and Harroff note that the most important characteristic of the Totally married was their approach to conflicting desires. Sometimes a compromise was reached, sometimes a compromise was avoided, sometimes one or the other had to give way, but both felt that the most important thing was their relationship. They *wanted* to preserve their relationship, at almost any cost.

"Ego economics" is only one of the ways by which total marriage can be threatened or destroyed. By examining the various causes of collapse of marriages we can see why Total marriages have exceptional inner strength.

XII
Total Support

The principal bases upon which Total marriages are built are mutual trust and respect. These people *each* feel that the other is the best of the two. Women's Lib to the contrary, the condition of servitude is not in physical externals but in internal feelings, and the latter does not follow necessarily or regularly from the former. Where each feels that they are serving the other, there is not a feeling of repression but one of self-realization. It is not a new idea that the highest state of man is *serving*.

The sense of being "supported" tends to make each partner more open and more willing to give support. It is, in engineering terms, a positive feedback system. Buckminster Fuller would call it a synergistic relationship.

In this system there will be output into the surrounding world. It takes place as work, love for children and friends, an enrichment of the ability to form strong and lasting friendships and a general sense of vitality.

Another base, that actually results from mutual trust and respect, is honesty. This is not the "phony" honesty that says I will not conceal my betrayals of you and of our relationship because that concealment would be dishonest. This is, rather, the honesty that springs out of a genuine feeling of wanting to be true to a commitment not only in word but in action. Totally married people are honest because they want to *share*, to share every thing they can ... together. That this kind of honesty will occasionally include criticism is clear. But what appears as criticism is also letting the other partner know clearly where he or she stands. It is a solid step toward avoiding the "secret contracts" that destroy so many marriages because neither partner is really sure of what their understanding is.

Clearly a rich sex life is also a solid part of any genuinely monogamous relationship. This is not to say that totally married people always are sexual athletes. People vary, genetically and by training, rather widely in their sexual needs and responses. But it does mean that the sexual relationship of deeply intimate people is accordingly deeply intimate. Whether actual intercourse takes place many times each week or once a month that intercourse will be characterized by a deep feeling of being together, a feeling of communication and a feeling of commitment to the partner.

The deprivation of sexual intimacy, through illness, old age, or temporary separation, seems to call forth the finest in human qualities, including a true sexuality. For if sexuality were limited to a physical act and to an "aura" before and after it, it would be meaningless to speak of the sexuality of children, of poetry, of religion. It is even conceiveable that a totally married couple could be celibate from start to finish. There are such cases on record, the human condition being as flexible as it is. Let us simply say that, when such relationships occur, the sexuality of each of the partners seems to be "sublimated" without depriving either of the feeling of intimacy that most of us can only realize with the "help" of sex. It is part of our animality.

XIII
When Monogamy Fails. . . .

The greatest threat to monogamy is a fear of commitment. The *inability* of either partner, not just the woman, to "surrender" his autonomy to the other will destroy or deeply cripple a monogamous relationship.

A corollary of fear of commitment, of course, is a fear of loss of any kind. One Total marriage broke up because the male partner suffered from a crippling disease. The wife, unable to stand the pain of actually feeling the wasting away of her husband's body, became unable to have sex with him and the marriage changed, in a very short time, to a Conflict-Habituated marriage. She could not leave him, he could not leave her, they were both frustrated and so they fought to retain some kind of intimate contact. That finally dissolved in frustration, and they lived out the remains of their lives in a Devitalized marriage.

Epilogue: Is Monogamy Obsolete?

A common cause of adultery is fear of personal failure. A man who is deeply threatened in his work will sometimes react by getting involved with a woman to whom he is not even deeply attracted. Whether this is a result of instinct or training, we don't know. Probably both forces are at work. But it is apparent that if a man is put in a position of stress and anxiety he is far more susceptible to the advances of women other than his mate than he is when he feels successful and secure.

The same force seems to operate with women. One young woman, happily married to a man with whom she was very much in love, discovered that she could never have children. The shock and sense of deprivation sent her on an orgy of promiscuity that lasted for nearly a year. She simply had to reinforce her feeling of being a woman, and infidelity was an unreasoned, automatic response.

Reasserting and reaffirming that you are attractive to the opposite sex seems to be a way that the human animal receives generalized reassurance.

Loss of personal involvement is the basic reason why adultery can be so destructive to a monogamous marriage. Adultery is almost always a dilution of commitment. No matter what kind of excuses are offered, adultery brings up the old threatening adage, "A husband is what a woman marries until the right man comes along." It is true for either sex, and it is a way of telling the partner that he or she does not satisfy the needs of the mate. In this sense it is also a demeaning insult and rightly arouses resentment. Who wants to be told, "You are not good enough for me?" For that is usually what adultery says. The other partner will inevitably feel, "If I were just better, just good enough, this would not have happened." Adultery is too often also an expression of anger toward the mate that cannot be voiced.

This is true, even when the mate never finds out. The adulterous partner is saying, deep inside, my mate is not good enough. And, on some level, they both know it. This is, of course, not the only reason why adultery damages a marriage, but it makes its effect felt subconsciously at all levels.

Pseudo-honesty is another great threat to monogamy. It is, almost always, a way of escaping responsibility for one's actions. This form of "honesty" is actually aggressive and hostile, because it forces the other person to accept a hurt without being able to respond properly. This is especially true when the "honesty" is the result of a personal contract with one's partner, acknowledged or implicit, that says "I will be honest with you but you must accept whatever that honesty brings, including my aggressions." The much mimicked film "Bob & Carol & Ted & Alice" shows the transformation from this type of honesty to a less mechanical, more humble honesty.

There is more cruelty committed in the name of honesty than ever happens when anger is freely acknowledged.

The question of jealousy and possessiveness is an important factor in any marriage. In *Open Marriage,* Nena and George O'Neill make a statement that contains both the crux of the usual argument against jealousy and a major example of the faulty reasoning that pervades the social sciences as a result of our rationalistic tradition.

"To begin with, we would like to lay to rest the idea that sexual jealousy is natural, instinctive and inevitable. It is none of those things. Jealousy is primarily a *learned* response, determined by cultural attitudes. In many societies around the world, including the Eskimo, the Marquesans, the Lobi of West Africa, the Siriono of Bolivia and others, jealousy is at a minimum; and in still others, such as the Toda of India, it is almost completely absent. If in other societies it is greatly reduced or hardly exists at all, then *it cannot be regarded as "natural" to man's behavior."* (Emphasis added.)

As the argument proceeds, it is claimed that jealousy is different from envy because jealousy involves the fear of losing something already possessed; and therefore it implies that sexual jealousy is based on the "bad" notion that one person owns another.

The first fallacy in the above argument is the assumption that what is natural to man must be true in *all* cases—again, the extension of rationalistic methods to human behavior. Simply because we can find a few examples among the myriad cultures of man that do not conform to the norm does not mean that the norm is not the "natural" and instinctive pattern. We repeat again that man is the most adaptable animal. Of course he can learn to repress this instinct just as well as he can so many others. In any study of human behavior, what exists in almost all cases is considered "natural." Furthermore, we can find many examples among pair-bonding animals of the lower orders where sexual jealousy *does* occur.

The second fallacy is that of ownership. Of course people can "own" each other ... as long as that ownership has been freely bestowed and *exchanged* for the ownership of the other partner, as it very often is. Therefore jealousy is the natural resentment aroused by a violation of the contract of mutual ownership.

We are also forced to the conclusion that jealousy is as natural an instinct as fear of death, sexual attraction, or crying as the result of being hurt. All of these reactions have been totally repressed in various cultures. That they are repressed does not mean that they are not "natural."

This is not to say that "bad" jealousy does not exist. Certainly it does. It is normally the result of either a deep feeling of lack of worth ... fear of lack of autonomy ... or the result of a fear of loss that is a substitution for a real loss in some other area of the person's life.

We can, with a little honest observation and common sense, distinguish between "healthy" jealousy and "sick" jealousy ... which, incidentally, is a danger to, but rarely occurs in, Total marriage.

The next great danger to monogamy is so much a part of the human condition that it must be treated separately.

XIV
Growing Out of Love

After extolling the wonders of Total marriages, we must also observe that they do not always last forever; indeed, it may be that they break up quite as often as the other types.

Life is growth and growth is change. When people, for whatever reason, change, the old rules must change or the contract is threatened. This is one of the reasons why Total marriages often have provisions for frequent discussion of change in the marriage. The physiology of man varies; men are not created equal. As we have seen, a disease can change the whole contract so radically that the contract is functionally voided, even when it remains in law.

There is no final answer to this question. Some Total marriages last until death because the will to make the marriage last is greater than the tendency to break the contract. Sometimes the directions or rates of growth are so different that the "perfect pair" of five years ago are like strangers to each other. This is one of the ways, mentioned by Cuber and Harroff, that marriage styles change. Cuber and Harroff actually discovered cases where Passive-Congenial marriages "grew" into Vital or Total marriages . . . or vice-versa.

Growth, as much as death and even more than taxes, we will always have with us. It is one of the reasons why there are no sure bets in the marriage game. The big question is, can growth be consciously guided in such a way a "seismic imbalance" can be avoided? Or is personal growth as uncontrollable as the physical pressures that produce an earthquake?

XV
The Monogamy of the Future?

It is an interesting comment on our society that most people in Total and Vital marriages conceal the fact from their friends. Cuber and Harroff quote several people who frankly stated that they didn't think their social circle would either understand or appreciate it if they knew how deep their love was. We might conjecture that it was a reasonable fear of envy and consequent hostility. "What would people say if they knew we were so happy?" I remember one couple in their fifties who were half embarassed to be discovered by a friend of their college-age son, necking on the living room couch.

This is an important difference between the "mature" generation and the young. Most of us over forty grew up in an age where love was nearly as private a thing as sex. There are many stories of children who knew their parents loved each other, but had never seen them embrace or kiss. Our American

Protestant ethic has been blamed for most of the evils of our age, and often unjustly, but there is no question about the blame here. The open display of love and affection was taboo.

The young are proud of their love and open in their display of affection as we never were. Along with their exploration of "new" areas of the spiritual, they are clearly discovering "new" ideas about the experience of joy in their own animality. They embrace each other, kiss each other, pat each other with an openness that is sometimes shocking and repulsive to many older people. And, in the process, they rid themselves of the adolescent fantasies so many of us still dream about.

While it can be argued, and the figures are not yet definitive, that there is little more sexual experimentation going on outside marriage now than there was twenty years ago, there can be no argument with the fact that it is more open.

I believe it is an extremely hopeful sign. The back seat of a car is a poor place to get to know someone as a whole human being.

To the degree that human animals are genuinely able to explore each other as complete human beings, they will be better able to make choices of lasting mates.

Recent statistics indicate that this is exactly what is happening. Marriages among young people 16 to 20 are sharply declining. The openness with which young people are now able to live together is preventing "passions of the moment" from becoming bad marriages. Nowadays, we can see all around us that young couples are frequently saying that they really like each other, but they don't want to get married until they have lived together for long enough to know that they can really weather the sacrifices of marriage.

Even twenty years ago it was largely the upper class that granted their children the right to explore their own bodies and the bodies, minds, and spirits of their peers. But the young have forced the issue. They have told their parents that they are going to live with other young people of their own age, either in pairs or in communal groups, and that is how it is going to be. The parents can either accept what is evident all around them, or they can "disown" their children, create needless hurt and sacrifice their children on the altar of pride.

Dr. Robert T. Francoeur, in his new book, *Eve's New Rib,* has examined the new "revolution in marriage" and concluded that the real revolution is taking place among the middle-aged and elderly. He feels that big changes in marriage are unlikely to come from the young because those who lean toward experimentation and change are trying communal living for a year or two and then leaving the communes and entering monogamous marriages. But isn't this a more basic revolution, after all?

We are entering upon a new age when marriage is going to be regarded as too important and too intimate to be the slave of sex. It is the most encouraging and hope-inspiring change in American mores for many decades.

Imagine marriage freed from the tyranny of sex. It is perfectly practical with today's attitudes and techniques, and it could save hundreds of young people from the insanity of jumping into marriage without the slightest idea of what it means to share their lives with another person.

It is a promise that can be realized if we are wise enough to stop worrying about it as an issue merely of "premarital sex." And it could well restore true monogamy as the basic mode of marriage in America.

XVI
Toward Compassion

Man is the most variable as well as the most adaptable animal on the earth. We are not born equal in talents, in disposition or physical attributes. It is unreasonable to expect that we are born equal in our ability to form pair-bonded marriages.

The enormous variability of marital customs in different cultures, and the relatively rapid changes in those customs in Western civilization, have not allowed any Darwinian "natural selection" to increase the survival of "naturally" pair-bonding individuals.

Cuber and Harroff discovered that many couples, not among the Vital or Total classifications of marital relationship, felt themselves to be happy. There are many couples who absolutely need to have extra-marital affairs. Whether by heredity or environment these people seem constitutionally unable to form a pair-bonded marriage.

Nothing in this epilogue is meant to condemn such people. They are what they are, and they merit respect as human beings.

The intent of this discussion is, rather, to examine the reasons why monogamy is far from moribund, and *to point out the obstacles that could be removed to make it easier for those who want to achieve it.* In our place and time, in our state of human development, monogamy is our best hope as a contract for love.